SAVING THE WORLD FROM YOUR HOME

SAVING THE WORLD FROM YOUR HOME

WHAT *One* PERSON CAN DO

P.H. Raynis

Our Sunday Visitor Publishing Division
Our Sunday Visitor, Inc.
Huntington, Indiana 46750

Copyright © 1987 by P.H. Raynis
ALL RIGHTS RESERVED

With the exception of short excerpts for critical reviews, no part of this book may be reproduced in any manner whatsoever without permission in writing from the publisher. Write:
Our Sunday Visitor Publishing Division
Our Sunday Visitor, Inc.
200 Noll Plaza
Huntington, Indiana 46750

International Standard Book Number: 0-87973-489-2
Library of Congress Catalog Card Number: 86-64001

Cover design by James E. McIlrath

PRINTED IN THE UNITED STATES OF AMERICA

ACKNOWLEDGMENTS: Most of the Scripture texts contained in this work are taken from the *Revised Standard Version, Catholic Edition,* © 1965 and 1966 by the Division of Christian Education of the National Council of the Churches of Christ in the U.S.A., all rights reserved. Biblical quotations excerpted from the *King James Edition of the Bible* (Thomas Nelson and Sons, n.d.) are identified by the letters KJ. Other sources from which material has been excerpted or has served as the basis for portions of this work include *The Screwtape Letters*, C.S. Lewis, Macmillan Publishing Co., Inc, New York, © 1972; *¡Gracias!*, Henry Nouwen, Harper and Row Pubs., Inc., San Francisco, © 1983; *Closed: 99 Ways to Stop Abortion*, Joseph M. Scheidler, Good News Pubs., Westchester, Ill., © 1985; *I, Catherine* [the letters of St. Catherine of Siena], ed. and trans. by Kenelm Foster and Mary John Ronayne, Collins Publishing, London, © 1980; *The Peace Catalog — A Guidebook to a Positive Future*, Press for Peace, Seattle, Wash., © 1984; and *Easy Essays*, Peter Maurin, Franciscan Herald Press, Chicago, © 1977. The author is grateful to the copyright holders for the use of their materials. If any copyrighted materials have been inadvertently used in this book without proper credit being given, please notify Our Sunday Visitor in writing so that future printings of this work may be corrected accordingly.

To Steven

Contents

introduction 9
{1} *why bother?* 13
{2} *getting started* 21
{3} *praying* 35
{4} *correspondence* 47
{5} *other writing* 65
{6} *using the phone* 73
{7} *hospitality* 85
{8} *other talents* 95
{9} *using money* 113
{10} *miscellaneous* 133
{11} *joining groups* 143
{12} *burnout* 155
{13} *conclusion* 165

introduction

Fifty years ago, it was known as Catholic Action.

Active Catholics were involved in helping others less fortunate than themselves in a variety of ways. Not only were they supporting the missions, but at home they fed the hungry in soup kitchens, marched with the oppressed in demonstrations, and helped out in hospitals and institutions as they could.

Today, Catholic Action has been changed to the "lay apostolate," and the Church is again urging its members to face tough current issues and do something about them.

The bishops' pastoral letters on peace and on the economy have mandated a radical evaluation of the average churchgoer's involvement in his society. Moreover, the letters have emphasized each person's responsibility for carrying out the works of Christ.

My own conviction that each person must work for the good of others began when I was in grade school, where we saved pennies for the missions.

My parents, especially my father, taught us that we had an obligation, both civic and religious, to help others. And there was always reading material around the house to reinforce that idea.

As time went on, and the nation went from the sleepy fifties to the anguished sixties, my sympathies, of course, were more directly engaged.

There were the anti-war movement and civil-rights struggles. We students, along with others who shared our concerns, marched in the streets, tutored inner-city kids in chilly church basements, and volunteered summer vacations away in the Appalachians.

But most of us weren't doing it all for the love of God and man, of course. We were just trying to redress what we saw as the crimes of the Establishment. And we were aiming toward a rather hazy concept of Utopia.

Like many others, though, I stepped back and regrouped in the 1970s. It was then I rediscovered my Catholic roots and started to get involved in volunteer work for the "right" reasons. This time, there was an added spiritual dimension to all of it, and that turned out to be the missing key from my earlier experiences.

About five years ago, my husband and I moved out into the country. Fifty miles away from the nearest city, and pretty much isolated on the farm, I began to feel a restlessness to work for justice again. But there were no organizations, no soup kitchens, no volunteer groups around. I grew frustrated and almost angry at the lack of opportunity to help.

It was then I began to seriously explore alternatives. I asked myself the following questions:

✓ What could I do alone, and at home?

✓ What did other people do?

✓ Was there any way to make a real impact on the world from the middle of nowhere?

I thought of the handicapped, confined to their wheelchairs; and I thought of the elderly, so often bound to apartments by illness or physical handicaps, or perhaps the lack of transportation, or the need to care for an ailing partner. Many, I knew, felt useless, but saw no way out of their circumstances.

I remembered young parents I'd talked to who often complained that they were wasting their lives because their freedom was restricted by lack of money for baby-sitters. They simply couldn't take off for rallies, speeches, or social actions without neglecting the family.

I even talked to many "nine to fivers" who rarely had time to spare for the "big" acts of mercy. Juggling job and home proved to be nearly all they could handle — but they confided in me that they really wanted to work for permanent changes in the system.

Then I thought of the residents of nursing homes. Many of them were still able to act for others, but they had no direction and little opportunity to use their abilities.

There had to be some answer for all of these "homebound."

This book is the result of that search. My discoveries, amazingly, were almost entirely positive. And I began to wonder what all those people who were "out in the field" were doing with their time!

It seemed that the real works of change and charity were being done by the quiet ones — those people who were based, either willingly or unwillingly, at home. And their contributions were invaluable. They were an integral part of the lay apostolate — not just part of the periphery.

I'd like to thank all those people and organizations who helped me during the research and writing of this book — especially those who shared their time and experiences so freely. Among them are Scott Rains of Prolifers for Survival, Toni Pepin from the National Wildlife Federation, and Bernard Broussard of Starthrowers.

To Susan Cable, Kathy Holmes, and Doris Wenig, who read and commented on this material, and to my morale boosters, Mary Ellen Urbanski-Gates, Jettie Graham, Treva Peterson, Sue Van Riper, Barbara Shaw, Maurya Smith, Sister Mary Grace, and to my mother, I owe special thanks.

Most of all, I must thank Steven T. Raynis, my husband. His patience, bribery, and general support helped me persevere when I was ready to quit.

1
why bother?

"And now the news..."

It's nearly always bad, and there's nearly always too much of it. Wars. Brutality. Crime. Pollution. Corruption in high places and low. Poverty. Injustice.

The whole lot's depressing, and many people, especially the homebound, feel hemmed in by the relentlessness of it.

These homebound include more than just the elderly and handicapped. They're also mothers with small children, those with seriously ill spouses or offspring, and rural dwellers with few social contacts. They're the people who can't get out to do much.

They watch or read the news and are disheartened with the rest, but their frustration has an added dimension. Even if they wanted to, they couldn't run soup kitchens, bind the wounds of victims, or march in rallies.

The result of all of this discouragement isn't action in most cases, though. It's paralysis.

"Why bother?" a person might ask himself. It's a good question. After all, what difference can one person possibly make, especially when he's shut off from the world?

C.S. Lewis recognized the syndrome in his book *The Screwtape Letters*. At one point, he has a senior devil instructing a junior, "Let him [the soul to whom the devil was assigned] do anything but act. . . . The more often he feels without acting, the less he will be able to act, and, in the long run, the less he will be able to feel."

So the news continues to be bad, and each injustice builds on another, while a hypnotized audience watches with disgust and growing despair — or, worse yet, sometimes with outright apathy.

* * *

Why bother trying to change things?

For one thing, no transformation can happen if there's no one to bring it about. The wrongs of the world won't be redressed if they're ignored. Deterioration will continue until it hits resistance.

Edmund Burke, the famous eighteenth-century statesman, counseled, "All that is necessary for the triumph of evil is for good men to do nothing."

In our own century, Martin Luther King, Jr., said,

"To ignore evil is to become an accomplice to it." While that's been demonstrated time and again, the most outstanding example involved the case of the Nazis in Germany in the period just prior to World War II.

The Nuremberg war trials pointed out that though not everyone participated in the horrifying crimes of Hitler's Third Reich, immense harm resulted from the fact that too few challenged those who *were* committing the evil. Citizens simply went along with the program at each stage until it was too late.

The Nuremberg Principles stated that it was a crime *not* to oppose immoral government policy. When a state orders actions that are clearly against moral law, they said, each person is responsible to act against it and try to change it.

The Catholic Church mandates the participation of its members in creating world justice. "Christ's faithful," Canon Law 222 states, ". . . are obliged to promote social justice and, mindful of the Lord's precept, to help the poor from their own resources."

Add to that the American bishops' pastoral letter, *The Challenge of Peace: God's Promise and Our Response*, which asserts, "Peacemaking is not an optional commitment. It is a requirement of our faith. We are called to be peacemakers, not by some movement of the moment, but by our Lord Jesus."

Even in the early days of the Church, the Desert Fathers emphasized the necessity of getting involved on some level when they wrote, "Remember, you will never arrive at a solution, but you are never absolved from the responsibility of trying."

The concept, however, that each man must act responsibly according to his beliefs goes all the way back to the Bible.

St. James, in his epistle, put it succinctly: "Be doers of the word and not hearers only" (James 1:22, KJ), while St. Paul wrote to the Galatians, "And let us not grow weary well-doing, for in due season we shall reap, if we do not lose heart" (Galatians 6:9).

When Paul was teaching in Corinth, he was instructed by God to "not be afraid, but speak and do not be silent; for I am with you" (Acts 18:9).

Jesus said: "Blessed are the peacemakers, for they shall be called sons of God.

"Blessed are those who are persecuted for righteousness' sake, for theirs is the kingdom of heaven" (Matthew 5:9-10).

Christ emphasized over and over again, in both His actions and words, the fact that we should love our neighbor enough to continually work for his welfare.

So it all crystallizes in the second commandment, "You shall love your neighbor as yourself." In working to create a peaceful, whole, and just world, we are doing exactly that. It is not just an option for a follower of Christ — it is a command.

We *must* bother.

* * *

What difference can one person possibly make?

Randall Forsberg, who is credited with starting the Nuclear Freeze Campaign, was an English teacher before she decided to devote her life to the cause of peace. After quitting the profession she'd held for years to work as a typist in a peace research institute, she developed and promoted her world-changing concepts.

Betty Williams and Mairead Corrigan were housewives in Northern Ireland when they decided to do something to stop the turmoil there. They formed the "Peace Community," which brought both Catholics and Protestants together in various actions for understanding and forgiveness. Because of their work, they won the 1976 Nobel Peace Prize.

Then there's John Banzhaf III, a young law student with no outside cash resources and no contacts, who conducted the campaign which eventually led to the removal of cigarette ads from TV.

Trevor Ferrell in his work for the homeless of Philadelphia, Candy Lightner in her efforts on behalf of the families of those killed by drunk drivers, and thousands of others, well-known and unknown, have influenced the world for the better in many degrees.

Most major changes have come about, as a matter of fact, from the efforts of individuals working "from the bottom up" rather than waiting for directives to come "from the top down."

The fact that an individual begins work alone, though, doesn't mean that he'll remain that way, or that his efforts are any less important than those of large, high-budget organizations.

For years, Ralph Nader worked solo to expose the dangers in the auto industry. Now, of course, his watchdog staffs are famous for protecting American consumers.

"I like to believe that people in the long run are going

to do more to promote peace than our governments. Indeed, I think that people want peace so much that one of these days governments had better get out of the way and let them have it!" That was President Dwight D. Eisenhower's answer when he was asked how effective it was for the people themselves to work for international relations.

His statement has been proven true most recently in the establishment of the National Peace Institute. The result of grass-roots efforts, it is the first official alternative to military colleges in the U.S.; funded by the government, its purpose is to teach the art of nonviolent solutions to international problems.

The Christophers, a national organization, encourages those who are alone to do what they feel is right and necessary to create a better world. The Christophers' motto says it all: "It is better to light one candle than to curse the darkness."

* * *

Aren't the homebound and the handicapped a different case, though? Don't they have enough to worry about without taking on the burdens of world peace and justice?

To the uncommitted world it might seem so. The fact that there are many who can't leave their homes because of illness, family obligations, or environmental isolation seems to exempt them from any expressions of social activism. The mobile of the world, in their misplaced pity for the homebound, tend to relegate them to the status of "cared for," rather than "caring." They are quick to release them from the responsibilities that the Gospels say they must shoulder as followers of Jesus.

Scott Rains, the director of Prolifers for Survival (a group recently disbanded), was asked what he felt the homebound could do for his group.

"I'm not sure just how 'homebound' you mean," he replied. "I manage to direct Prolifers for Survival, serve on the board of directors of Just Life PAC and travel around the country — and I am a quadraplegic!"

Studying the ways of working for peace and justice in depth clearly shows that the bulk of the work that needs to be done in order to really effect changes can easily be accomplished at home. The day-to-day, unspectacular jobs that put pressure on entrenched politicians and bureaucrats to change their disastrous courses aren't necessarily best done in the field.

Much of the problem is one of attitude.

To believe in Christ means to believe that nothing is without purpose. So our outward circumstances don't exempt us from Christian charity — they merely direct its expression. Because there's a place for those who live in quiet surroundings, with plenty of flexible time, and because there's a niche for those who can sympathize with the suffering, there's a spot in the scheme of things for the homebound.

* * *

How can anyone know where to begin?

Dorothy Day — who, with Peter Maurin, founded the Catholic Worker Movement — answered that question with another: "How are you going to overcome wars unless you begin right where you are?" And that's the crux of the matter.

A news article stirs us. A TV story enrages us. A radio spot moves us to pity. They're all starting points. The places we need to work are found in the events that touch our hearts.

Just as a mother who sees her child being kidnapped by a band of thugs won't simply wring her hands and watch them go — hoping that someone, somewhere, sometime, will do something about it — so must we do whatever is in our power to correct unjust and dangerous situations. The techniques we use depend greatly on our talents, inclinations, and abilities. But the fact of our involvement should be a given.

"The future will be different," Peter Maurin assured his listeners, "if we make the present different."

Action breeds action, as indicated in the quote from *The Screwtape Letters* earlier in this chapter, and success stimulates success. We must begin somewhere, if we're not to remain stuck in the glue of inertia.

No one's exempt, no one's excused.

RESOURCES*

The Christophers, 12 East 48th St., New York, NY 10017

---

*Where applicable, RESOURCES will be included at the end of each chapter, with some being repeated as necessary. (RESOURCES are some of the recommended groups and individuals to contact in your efforts to "save the world from your home.")

2
getting started

Once the fire's laid, it's wise to decide where the smoke will escape before actually lighting a flame.

And once we're convinced of the need to work for the betterment of the world, we should determine where we're going to put our energies before we start billowing off in all directions. Burning out with nothing to show for it but charred nerves helps no one.

* * *

Our first job, then, should be to get focused.

Although nearly every aspect of life on this planet

needs some sort of improvement, most people are only attracted to certain areas of interest. Such attractions can cue us as to where we'll be able to work most effectively.

Take the peace issues, for example.

There are many ways of promoting peace in the world, all with the aim of easing tensions and reducing the possibility of war. Those who are interested in such global visions can work on campaigns that increase international understanding, oppose nuclear weapons, or fight terrorism. Others may want to apply their efforts to narrower fields, such as supporting peace actions in Northern Ireland or other international hot spots. There are others yet who may choose to get involved in politics or work against the spread of Communism.

Pope Paul VI said, "If you wish peace, work for justice."

Those who opt to work for a just and equitable world have a myriad of issues that scream for their attention. All of the following are equally important, equally critical.

Hunger	Housing
Human rights	Women's rights
Prison reform	Life questions
Universal health care	Religious discrimination
Consumer protection	Age discrimination
Handicapped rights	Abused children protection
Pornography	Violence
Crime	Minority rights
Farming questions	Media responsibility
Education	Refugee questions

But that's not all! There's a whole range of environmental issues that need to be addressed by those who are supposed to be stewards of God's earth. For people concerned in these fields, some of the most outstanding areas open to work are: wildlife protection, the establishment of nature preserves, the conservation of natural resources, pollution control, and the protection of animal rights.

But if none of those questions really intrigue us, we may find that we're sparked by the idea of working for Church reform and renewal with such projects as liturgy work, evangelization, building community, or educating the young in the traditions and doctrines of the faith.

A lot of the above overlap, of course, and though our primary interest might be, for example, human rights, we may find that we spend a lot of time on efforts involving religious discrimination and prison reform as well. But by deciding initially where our hearts are, we'll find that we're able to do justice to more than one area because we're coming out of a center.

One philosopher urged his readers: "Think globally. And act locally."

In searching for significant commitments, no one should overlook local questions. They're usually the most responsive to individual effort, and they tend to touch each person most directly. Though, at first glance, local problems may not seem as important as national or international issues, they are the major components that make up the overall climate of a nation.

In determining our area of focus, it's helpful to choose to work *for* an ideal rather than *against* an abuse. It leads to a more positive outlook, and gives us a worthy goal to look toward. We should try concentrating on building, rather than destroying — loving, rather than hating.

It's essential, finally, to remember that no one field of concern is any less important than another. In the long run, each adds to the general goal of a peaceful, whole, and just world.

* * *

Mother Teresa of Calcutta was once approached by a group of activists who chided her because she wasn't really working to change the corrupt systems that led to all of the poverty she was trying to alleviate. The people, they said, would be better off if they were taught rather to organize and overcome their oppressors than to merely try to get enough to eat.

"That's not our charism," she replied. "It's better that each follow the way God has given them. . . . You have your work; I have mine. God will bless us both if we do them well."

Focusing is the process by which we find out where God wants us to work. And self-evaluation is the tool that helps us discover how we're to go about it most effectively. Together, they combine to form what Mother Teresa called a "charism."

Mother Teresa cares for the sick skillfully. She inspires others to do the same.

Thomas Merton wrote well. He was able to stimulate others with his deep thinking.

And Sister Corita made lovely posters. She stirred the hearts of a nation with them.

There are more talents than writing, painting, and tending the sick, though, that can be used to make the world a more just and peaceful place. Some of them spring immediately to mind, while others are quieter and often go unrecognized.

A partial list of such skills, both common and uncommon, follows.

Writing	Painting
Reading	Researching
Organizing	Being hospitable
Caring for animals	Poster making
Speaking	Craftwork
Listening	Teaching
Cooking	Typing
Sewing	Running a computer
Gardening	Inspiring others
Using office skills	Talking on the phone

All of these lend themselves to a variety of projects, and none of them are the exclusive property of the mobile. Homebound people can use them as effectively as others.

Our next move, then, is to find out where our talents lie, and which actions appeal to us most. Three questions can help direct our vision:

√ What do I do well?
√ What do I like to do?
√ What do others say I do well?

By meditating on them, we may find our particular path to effective action. And as soon as they're answered thoughtfully, we're really ready to begin.

* * *

Once we've focused our interests and abilities, we need to educate ourselves for effective action.

If we expect to be able to answer the questions and comments of others capably, we must be well-versed in our field. It's not only embarrassing but also ineffectual to be caught without adequate foundation for a passionately held belief.

The facts we learn, as well as the conclusions we draw from them, aren't just for our own use either.

"Decision making in the United States relies upon a well-informed citizenry. . . . It is the right and even the responsibility of American citizens to investigate issues of importance and then to tell their public officials what course to take. A free flow of information works only to the benefit of a democracy," write the editors of *The Peace Catalog*.

But we needn't become award-winning experts in our field. Just having a sound background and being familiar with current developments is often enough. It is here that the homebound have the advantage over many others. In-depth research takes a great deal of time, and that, in most cases, is the strong suit of those who aren't able to get out.

There are ways to cut research time, though. Being focused is one of them. Because we are dealing in one area only, our required reading is necessarily limited. And because we've chosen our own field, we're necessarily more interested in what we're reading, thus leading to faster work.

A person who is fascinated with the question of wildlife preservation, for instance, may be totally bored with the politics of housing in the United States, even though that's an important question in its own right. And because he yawns at the prospect of reading about dislocation and housing starts, he won't be able to really concentrate and will probably abandon the project early on.

But when presented with the migratory patterns of the caribou and facts related to that animal's preservation during its yearly travels, the same person will come alive and likely will be stimulated to write to governments and hunting lobbies in an effort to save dwindling caribou numbers. And action, after all, is the purpose of getting involved.

What are the best ways to get this education?

Magazines and newspapers are great places to start. Once our field of interest is determined, stories and articles regarding it will seem to pop out at us as we read. Clipping pertinent material and filing it is very helpful for later reference.

There are thousands of periodicals published regularly in the United States. Most are targeted at specialized audiences, though a few of them are of general interest. It's valuable to subscribe to those that concentrate on our field, because they not only have important articles and columns, but they also run ads and announcements for other sources that will be helpful to us.

Many organizations put out regular newsletters that are very enlightening in specific areas. They're usually free to members, or inexpensive for others, and are well worth the cost. Moreover, they're often a fine way to keep up-to-date on local or specialized developments, and can add depth to regular coverage by the media.

Sometimes reading journals that hold opposing viewpoints will help us to clarify our thoughts. These periodicals may present issues and facts with which we weren't familiar. They may force us to face our own prejudices. Or they may strengthen us in our convictions and make us better able to teach them to those who are interested. By knowing the arguments against our stand, we grow more well-rounded in our education.

For a deeper and more enduring treatment of our topic than magazines can give, we must turn to books. They can express wider ranges of opinions than periodicals because they need not fit a preset format and editorial bias.

Books can be obtained through bookstores, mail-order outlets, and libraries. Many of these last can request locally unavailable titles through an inter-library loan network. For those who can't leave home, mail-order and library-delivery service are the most practical way of getting reading material.

Radio and TV are a great help in getting general information quickly. However, they are often quite biased, and must be evaluated as such; but even at that, they present the latest developments and some in-depth reports very palatably.

For those who have cable TV, public-access channels are a help in examining local issues, and even the proceedings of Congress are carried on one generally available station.

* * *

"I'll Vote On" is a twelve-minute documentary videotape that examines U.S. Department of Justice action against civil-rights activists in black areas of the deep South where white political power is threatened. Rental: ten dollars.

"Las Nicas" is a forty-five-minute videotape in which Nicaraguan women speak about work, sexual politics, religion, family life, children, social participation, and military defense. Rental: seventy-five dollars for one week.

Just as videotapes have taken over the entertainment world, they've also become more and more popular in the field of education at home, as is seen by the ads in one issue of a social-justice magazine mentioned above. For those with the proper equipment, they provide an enjoyable educational alternative to reading or watching scheduled commercial broadcasts.

Audiotapes are wonderful ways to "attend" lectures, seminars, and classes, too. Often a student or listener attending them will tape them and will be happy to lend the tapes out. And many times, seminars are recorded by those who run them. These tapes are then sold or rented for a modest fee to those who are unable to be there. Several publications advertise home-study tapes that are very valuable for those who are homebound.

Sharing groups are excellent places to swap opinions and acquire new information. Sometimes "brainstorming" with others about a problem will bring out little-known facts and exciting possibilities. These groups can be hosted by the homebound and thus be quite accessible to all.

It's very important to remember, as Bruce Rahtjen points out in his book, *Scripture and Social Action*,

"Any social action which we must undertake must be theologically sound in terms of our doctrine of Christ."

We can't overlook the need to examine issues in that light, both through the religious press and church-related study programs. Reading the Bible and commentaries on it, as well as investigating the papal encyclicals and bishops' pastoral letters, will help greatly in keeping on a sound path of action.

* * *

Once we've focused our interests, evaluated our talents, and begun to educate ourselves in our particular field, we're ready to begin our concrete preparations for action.

For most people, that will mean setting aside, if possible, a desk or table where they can work at any time.

Correspondence will require paper and pens, pre-stamped postcards, envelopes, and stamps, as well as an address book or notebook with pertinent addresses (such as governmental representatives, newspapers, magazines, and television and radio stations).

Reference material should be kept handy also so that a minimum of time and effort will be spent searching for facts that are necessary to back up opinions. Dictionary, almanac, file folders of clippings from newspapers and magazines, and other pertinent books are good basic resources.

Those who choose to do phone work should keep a note pad, pens, phone books, and special phone-number books convenient to the telephone.

For arts and craftwork, the appropriate materials can be stored in a well-lighted area where it's comfortable to work, and where they won't have to be set up separately each time. It helps to have an idea book in the area for sketching or working out new concepts.

Whichever supplies are needed, if they're kept organized and handy, they will be great incentives to spend time actually working on projects, rather than feeling guilty about needing to do something "sometime."

* * *

Gandhi said, "The best propaganda is not pamphleteering, but for each of us to try to live the life he would have the world to live."

In order to do this, we need to examine our customary attitudes and develop those that will most benefit others.

First, we should be prepared to begin work even if we don't think we're entirely ready.

There's a great temptation to succumb to the "paralysis of analysis," but we must realize that no one's education is ever finished. So it's better to write a letter, or make a poster, or call a representative, than to sit silently by while others are suffering. Though we need to present our facts as well as possible, we should always be willing to go beyond our timidity to help those who depend on us.

Next, it's essential to "think small" when starting.

Even if we're just working from our living rooms, we're very likely to become overambitious and try to save the world in a single bound. It's better to avoid premature discouragement, to break our intentions down into a series of lesser goals.

If the end result is to feed the homeless, for example,

a viable smaller goal might be to provide supplies for the food banks, soup kitchens, and other food-distribution points that are already doing that. A workable beginning project may be to collect food for them from those in the neighborhood who can afford to give. And one way to do that is to phone everyone on the block or in the apartment building, or make flyers to be handed out at every door by a volunteer.

Each end attained leads us with more confidence on to the next one — and each step taken encourages us to continue, while bringing us closer to our vision. Greater actions will come as we are ready for them.

Be optimistic! The bad news of the media and the discouraging words of neighbors aren't final. Idealists have always been called fools, but St. Paul urged us to be "fools for Christ." And Gandhi said that no matter how insignificant the action we do may seem, it is important that we do it.

Keep in mind that less than one hundred fifty years ago there was still slavery in the U.S., and some said it would never be otherwise. Its abolition was the result of many individuals working against very stiff odds. Today's goals are no more difficult to effect.

A good working partner to optimism is patience. Major changes take time. Perseverance isn't a modern virtue, nor a popular one, but it can outlast any problem. And it can keep us sane in the maelstrom.

A worker for peace and justice must be trusting. The works of mercy require that we trust those with whom we talk, to whom we extend our hospitality, and with whom we work. There is no place for fear or suspicion in those who've committed themselves to this work.

We *will* be used. We *will* be taken advantage of from time to time. But so was Christ, and the others who've followed Him. We must be prepared for that and learn to discount it.

And with trust we must cultivate the quality of "openness."

Peter Maurin, who founded the Catholic Worker Movement with Dorothy Day, was often mistaken for a bum. Because he dressed shabbily and tended to be untidy, he was more than once shown to the kitchen door at places where he'd been invited to be a lecturer. In one professor's home, the maid showed him to the cellar, assuming he was a plumber, and he wasn't rescued by the host until hours later!

So we must remain open to other people, even though they may not appear to be "our type." Their ideas may be just what we need to break through our habits of thought, and they could have exactly what we need to learn. Understanding and empathy are essential, too, because no person is merely an adversary or a subject for us to work on. Each one is a human being and must be treated as such. That, indeed, is what peace and justice are all about.

A great antidote to both distrust and closed-mindedness is a sense of humor. Without it, no worker can continue, and it keeps us all from becoming too self-important, too wound up in our own plans for the world.

* * *

Then at last, being focused, educated, equipped, and

having a proper attitude, we're ready to breathe deeply, pray silently for guidance, and begin working for peace and justice!

RESOURCES

Independent Scholarship Project, 17 Myrtle Dr., Great Neck, NY 11021 (Encourages independent scholarship techniques and teaches them.)

3
praying

    For the sake of the thirty-six, God extends His mercy to the world.

    It's an ancient Hasidic belief that there are thirty-six saintly men in each generation for whom God spares the world. They're called the Zaddikim and they offer constant prayer and suffering to plead for his pity on their sinful world. They usually assume the guise of poor workmen so that even those around them won't know who they are.

    Even today, at least one modern theologian has wondered about the idea.

"Why does God still allow this world to continue?" Henri Nouwen writes in his book ¡Gracias! "Because of Ronald Reagan, Begin, Brezhnev, Thatcher, Marcos, Belaunde or Torrelio? Or perhaps because of the few hermits hidden in the forests of Russia, on the roofs of New York City and in the favelas of Brazil, Peru and Bolivia? When the Lord looks down on us, what does He see?"

In Christian tradition, these pray-ers (that is, those who pray as opposed to the actual prayers themselves) are called intercessors, and they either live in the world actively, or are cloistered away in hidden monasteries. Whichever they choose, they devote themselves to praying and sacrificing for others who cannot or will not pray for themselves.

St. Paul, in his letter to Timothy, said, "I exhort, therefore, that first of all, supplications, prayers, intercessions, and giving of thanks be made for all men; for kings and for all that are in authority; that we may lead a quiet and peaceable life in all godliness and honesty" (1 Timothy 2:1-2, KJ).

Those who are homebound have a special opportunity to engage in this type of ministry and should consider it seriously.

The main requirements of being an intercessor are commitment and time. Because those who are confined to home often have at least the flexibility to schedule in a regular prayer time, they are in a unique position to accept the important position of mediator.

The work is hard, and it requires a great deal of effort. It's not spectacular in the eyes of the media or the world in general. And there's no specific end to it, as there is in dressing the wounds of a dying man or serving soup to a line of hungry down-and-outers. Even the results, when they happen, are misattributed. Success is usually ascribed to the visible doers and not their spiritual "backups."

But as hidden and thankless as it may be, an intercessor's work is sometimes recognized for the value that it has. St. Teresa of Lisieux, the Little Flower, lived a cloistered life in Carmel from the age of fifteen, and never did travel in the world except when she went to see the pope in Rome to beg his permission to join the convent. Yet, she's been named the "Patroness of the Missions."

Why?

Because she offered her sacrifices and prayers for the missioners in foreign lands. She was often tempted with the thought that she was "wasting" her life behind the grille and that she should be out teaching and converting others for Christ. But she offered even these desires to Him. Although she never knew the results of her prayers, she continued them, knowing by faith that they would strengthen and supplement the works of those who were out in the field.

Vince Eirene wrote in the *Catholic Agitator*, "The works of mercy, serving the poor, and resisting the military are something you can fake. You could be doing it because of ego reasons, and . . . put on a show. But . . . the work of prayer, Christ says, . . . is something we cannot fake."

Today, those "on the front lines" are begging for

prayers like Teresa's from those who are in a position to offer them. Joe Scheidler, a pro-life leader, writes in *Closed: 99 Ways to Stop Abortion*, "We must pray for the perseverance of pro-life activists. We must pray for mothers. We must pray for abortionists. We must pray for the unborn. We must become Prayer Warriors."

There are a number of ways to live a life that meets the mandate and demand for prayer. Some of them are solitary efforts, while others use the support system of a group.

WORKING WITH ORGANIZED PRAYER MINISTRIES • Before she met Mother Teresa in 1948, Jacqueline de Decker, a Belgian lay woman, had been working with Calcutta's poor for many years. She, like the foundress of the Missionaries of Charity, had been caring for the "poorest of the poor" with little thought of herself.

But soon after their meeting, Jacqueline de Decker had to return to Belgium, and never returned to India.

She'd had a diving accident when she was fifteen, and the results began to show up drastically during her grueling years of service. She began a long series of operations (to date she has had over thirty), and had to learn to survive with collar and iron corset, walking with crutches.

In 1949, she received a letter from Mother Teresa with an exciting concept. She was to become the first of a group of people who would provide prayer support for the missionaries in the field.

"I want especially the paralyzed, the crippled, the incurables to join. How happy I am to have you all. . . . You are a Treasure House, the Power House of the Missionaries of Charity," Mother Teresa wrote to her and those who followed her, after the "Sick and Suffering" — as they came to be known — were formed.

Today, there are groups of Sick and Suffering Co-Workers of Mother Teresa in nearly every nation. Each member is assigned a nun or brother, and agrees to write to him or her twice a year, at Christmas and Easter. The members pray for the nuns or brothers, daily, and offer their sufferings for them. They also try to live in the spirit of the active missionaries, which means in joy, trust, and poverty.

Membership in this group is not limited to those who suffer physically. Some mothers with retarded or helpless children have become members, and have offered both their pain and that of their children for the sisters and brothers. And that idea can be extended to those caring for the adult helpless, such as those who have Alzheimer's disease.

A variation of Mother Teresa's idea has been used in Chicago by the Ministry of Praise.

In 1979, Sister Mary Charla Gannon started what came to be known as the Ministry of Praise among the elderly and homebound with whom she worked. Noticing that many of these people were not only lonely, but felt useless and left out of parish life, she researched ways of integrating them into a whole participation in the Body of Christ. She proposed a network for them by which they would back up all parish activities and needs through prayer.

From a small cadre of seventy-five members in one

parish, the movement has grown to encompass fifteen dioceses in the United States and currently has over eight thousand members.

In those parishes where the program has been started, the results have been noticeable. Confessions among those who haven't been inside a church in years have risen; increased participation in church activities among young people and other encouraging signs have been remarked on by both priests and the people.

Like the Sick and Suffering Co-Workers of Mother Teresa, those who join the Ministry of Praise promise to offer their prayers and sacrifices for the good of others. But instead of supporting a single brother or nun, they volunteer their blessings for the good of their parish and the Church in general.

Other groups, such as Fellowship in Prayer (which prays for world peace) and the Apostolate of Suffering (which offers daily pain and sorrow for the good of others), encourage prayer support and intercession for a number of causes.

FORMING OTHER NETWORKS OF PRAYER • There's a strong attraction in the idea of praying with other people for peace, missionaries, or the Church. Joining a group provides a sense of community and strength that comes from working together for a single purpose. And associating for the practice of prayer is doubly beneficial because of its sanction by Christ when He said, "For where two or three are gathered in my name, there am I in the midst of them" (Matthew 18:20).

But often, pray-ers feel prompted to respond to other

needs, some of them very local and specific in nature. Though they'd like to have the support of a group, many can't find one that serves their requirements.

The answer may be to begin a "Spiritual Network" of their own. By letting people know of their concerns and how they hope to deal with them, they may find that they're not "crying in the wilderness" at all. Some — perhaps homebound, too — may have been waiting for an explorer to show the way. As Sister Gannon found, there is a great deal of prayer energy waiting to be tapped by those who can organize it.

St. Clare's Parish in Albany, New York, for example, has an association of prayer sponsors for its religious-education program. Each member is assigned a grade and remembers it and its teacher during the daily prayer time, as well as at the time the class is held, if possible.

The best way to form a network is to talk about it with friends who might be interested. Eventually, two or three may join together in praying for the same purpose. Then a notice inserted in the church bulletin or a local newspaper may bring a lot of response from those who've been touched by the idea.

Groups can be very loose or quite formal, depending on their purpose and the nature of those who belong to them. Some are meant to be temporary (such as those formed to pray for striking workers) while others are in for the long haul (such as those dedicated to praying for the abortion issue). Whichever they are, though, a couple of practices tend to keep the members active and involved.

The first is regular communication. That will build

the sense of community needed to continue a strong prayer program, and will let those who belong know that their efforts are appreciated.

Writing a short monthly newsletter to all the members (it helps to have someone who can photocopy it) both reminds them of the commitment they've made and keeps them up-to-date on the state of the issue. If there's any positive news to pass on, the letter is the place to do it. It's easier to continue praying for something if one can see results from time to time!

The second thing is to have a specific prayer that each member agrees to say each day. Such a prayer serves to unify the partners as well as to give them an identity. Handing out prayer cards with the devotion printed on it will help to encourage participation, too, as the member can put it in a convenient spot as a reminder. The prayer can either be a well-known one, such as the Co-Workers' Peace Prayer of St. Francis, or one that was composed by a member of the network.

However the group is organized, it's important not to overload members with requirements. Asking only for a short period of prayer for the purpose, or just to say the network's prayer once a day, is enough. Many will give far more time than the minimum. But those who don't have the extra hours may feel guilty if they consistently can't fulfill their commitment, and will drop out soon after joining.

An important point is to start small and personal. Large numbers aren't required to accomplish great deeds. Desire and commitment are the most important elements in carrying on the work of intercession, which is the purpose of "Spiritual Networks." And they do have great value. As Mother Teresa has said, "There is a tremendous strength that is growing in the world through this continual sharing, praying together, suffering together and working together."

One interesting variation on this theme is the "Perpetual Rosary" group started by Bernadette Pederson in Washington. In it, volunteers sign up for one time each week to say the rosary for the conversion of Russia. That way, the prayer is being said continually.

PRAYING ALONE • Groups and networks aren't the only way to go, though.

There's definitely a place in the tradition of the Church for those who pray alone. The Desert Fathers were prime examples of those who interceded in solitude and made a tremendous difference in a secular and decaying world, not unlike our own.

Today, many feel hesitant to commit themselves to regular prayers and sacrifice because they're afraid they'll be unfaithful. And others don't really want to bind themselves to a single cause.

Fortunately, there are practices that will help these people to channel their prayer constructively as well.

One of them is the use of the "prayer calendar."

This is simply an appointment calendar that's marked with special dates, including birthdays, anniversaries, weddings, operations, exam days for friends and relatives, starting dates for new jobs, etc. It can be hung by the telephone, which makes it easy to mark as soon as a call is completed. Or, it can be placed near a favorite quiet corner or next to the bed as a reminder to pray for the people concerned when the event occurs.

A prayer calendar can be more universal, too. Dates of national and local elections and votes can be noted on it, as well as anniversaries of general importance, such as the Fourth of July or Hiroshima Day. Marking international occurrences such as peace conferences and papal visits is a good idea, too, because by remembering them in prayer, we become an intimate part of these important happenings.

Another practice is to "adopt" a public figure for prayer support.

Nearly a year before she entered Carmel, St. Teresa of Lisieux "adopted" Pranzini, a criminal who was condemned to be hanged for committing three brutal murders. By all accounts, he was unrepentant, stating that he was innocent of the crime, though it was proven that he led a life of habitual crime, and was well known as a seducer of women.

Once she'd read of him in the papers, Teresa made herself responsible for him, and prayed and sacrificed daily for his salvation.

He refused to confess even on the morning of his execution, and mounted the scaffold silently. As he put his head under the blade of the guillotine, he suddenly asked a nearby priest for his crucifix, and kissed it three times!

Teresa said of this, "I had obtained the sign I asked for, . . . to encourage me to pray for sinners." And she referred to Pranzini as her "first child," having Masses said for the repose of his soul, until her death ten years later.

There are many today who can use the same sort of "adoption." Media personalities, leaders of countries, and criminals all need someone to hold them up before God compassionately. They really are often the "forgotten ones" who need someone to honestly care for them, even though they may not ever know who their benefactors are.

A third exercise is that of fasting.

Fasting can be done privately or publicly, in protest of conditions (such as the hunger strikes of the suffragettes), in reparation for corporate sin (as Israel did under Samuel), or both (as Gandhi did during the riots of Calcutta).

In their now-famous peace pastoral, *The Challenge of Peace: God's Promise and Our Response*, the U.S. bishops called for American Catholics to resume the practice of Friday fast and abstinence. They recognized both the need for an individual discipline to be offered for the good of all, and the fact that abstaining from food does make those who do it more sensitive to the promptings of the Spirit.

Though many who are homebound because of handicaps may not be able to accomplish a full fast from all food, they may find that they can refuse themselves special treats for a stated period of time, or complete a partial fast for a day. And those actions can be just as valuable as any other form of denial.

* * *

So the field is wide open today for those who are willing to pray, fast, and sacrifice for the good of all. Though it's a tall order, the homebound can fill it perhaps better than any other single group.

RESOURCES

- *Apostolate of Suffering*
  Sacred Heart Center, 1022 S. Jackson St., Louisville, KY 40203

Fellowship in Prayer, 134 Franklin Corner Rd., Lawrenceville, NJ 08648

- *Ministry of Praise*
  Sister Mary Charla Gannon, SRM, St. Bede the Venerable Church, 8200 S. Kostner Ave., Chicago, IL 60652

- *Perpetual Rosary*
  Bernadette Pederson, Rt. 1, Box 229, Medical Lake, WA 99022

- *Sick and Suffering Co-Workers of Mother Teresa*
  Mary Kay Gormley, 533 Cloverleaf Dr., Minneapolis, MN 55422

  Barbara Florence, 205 Rhode Island Ave. S., Golden Valley, MN 56426

4
correspondence

She was a bold woman, that Catherine of Siena! Among all her other activities, she took priests, cardinals, and even two popes (Gregory XI and Urban VI) to task for the terrible state the Church was in. Letter after letter she sent — and got some satisfying results.

"I desire to see you a real man, fearless and making no concessions to self-love...," she wrote to Gregory XI, urging him to return the papacy from Avignon to Rome. "For I believe," she continues in *I, Catherine*, "and see in the sight of God that this more than anything else is keeping you back from your good and holy desire and thwarting the honor of God and the exaltation and reform of holy Church."

The art of effective letter-writing didn't die with her, though. It can be engaged in productively by even ordinary citizens today.

For those who want to do something to change the world, the incentive to begin corresponding is great. Political letters can sway votes, open the way for new legislation, and help establish priorities for elected officials.

One letter is worth one hundred voters. At least that's how the staffs of most government representatives count it. So just by sending a letter to the proper person, a writer automatically becomes a spokesman for one hundred constituents without ever having been elected! And because ninety-nine percent of all Americans don't write to their congresspeople about anything, they leave those who do with a great deal of power — and responsibility.

Warren Cassidy, a well-known lobbyist, has said, "When people write, Congress listens." And according to the Citizen's Policy Center, "Congressional aides say ten letters or phone calls will get the representative's attention and could swing his or her vote."

Being prepared is important in this ministry. It's essential to keep stocked up with stationery, stamps, writing implements, and pre-stamped postcards so that our response to any given situation can be prompt and timely. And if these materials are kept out on their own desk or corner of a table, they'll be spurs to greater and greater efforts.

It's not necessary to have fancy stationery or an expensive typewriter to correspond effectively. Clean, neat letters on lined paper are always given close attention by any staff.

A vital part of this work is knowing how to put an effective letter together. There are a few rules to follow that will help a letter have more impact, and will make the job of composing it easier.

1. Know who to write to. In most cases, if a problem is national or international in scope, the best people to correspond with would be Federal congressmen (or congresswomen), including the local House of Representatives member, and both senators. Sometimes, though, letters will be more efficient if they go to the head of a committee where a bill is being considered or debated.

People often become confused when their concerns are regional or local ones. For those, the correct persons to contact will be state, county, or municipal authorities.

Getting the right person may take a bit of research at first, but it will gradually become easier as we grow more familiar with the routine.

2. Spell names correctly. It's hard for a politician to take a writer seriously when he neglects to check the basic facts of address. Misspelling indicates lack of thought and often causes the receiver to view the writer negatively.

3. Begin with a compliment. No matter who the official is or how the writer personally feels about him, he must have done something worthwhile during his term of office! Try to ferret that out and begin the letter on a positive note.

4. Be courteous. Because they're unpleasant to read, abusive letters don't get much attention, and unsigned ones are tossed in the trash.

5. Be current. If a bill is being considered, it's best to write about it from two weeks to four days before its scheduled vote.

Pre-stamped postcards come in handy if there's no time to put together a complete presentation. Although it's difficult to write a thorough note on a postcard, it's better to get out some reaction than to remain silent at momentous times.

6. Write personally. Don't try to parrot brochures or form letters. Communication is weighed more heavily if it's in the words of the person who wrote it, and doesn't look like part of a mass-mailing campaign.

7. Have a point and come to it. Starting informally shouldn't open the floodgates to personal rambling. Few legislative aides (who will most likely be the ones to read a letter) have time to wade through several paragraphs of irrelevant information. They need to be able to grab the main idea and answer that, or put the facts at the disposal of their boss for further study.

And always refer to a bill by its correct number ("HR No. ___" for the House of Representatives and "S No. ___" for the Senate), if at all possible.

8. Be brief. Limit each letter to one topic and deal with that exclusively, unless it's intimately bound up with another. If the latter is the case, tie the two issues together from the start and address them as one.

9. State the reasons for your opinions. This is where the preliminary steps of education and research come in

handy. Most public figures are impressed by writers who know the facts that support their stands and who can give them clearly. Often, new information will be welcome, as it's impossible for any office holder to be knowledgeable about all topics.

Personal experience counts for a lot when it's used to back up opinions. Don't hesitate to include any firsthand knowledge you may have on a topic in your presentation.

10. Ask questions. Inquiries serve two purposes. First, they clarify the authority's position on a subject and force him to be public about it. And second, they encourage an answer, opening the way to an ongoing correspondence.

11. Write regularly. Many politicians have been influenced by constituents who've "adopted" them for a particular reason. By corresponding once a month or so, writers have established meaningful dialogue and kept their representatives aware of and updated on developments in a particular field of interest.

One part of this ongoing exchange should be the use of "thank you" notes when a representative votes in accordance with the writer's wishes. It both reinforces and encourages positive action on that and future actions.

So senators, representatives, and state legislators are prime targets for political letters. But on a local level, even school boards and administrations can be very responsive to taxpayers' comments and suggestions.

One woman in Tucson, Arizona, for example, learned that the health classes in her children's large public high school included abortion as an alternative to pregnancy, without stressing other options for unwed mothers. She and her husband began to write letters and phone officials advocating equal time for pro-life speakers. And before the end of the semester, that time was granted.

Letters like hers might be used to correct problems, or to add to the school schedule various classes or lectures that might otherwise be left out.

When suggesting lectures, it's helpful to suggest available speakers or organizations for the board to contact. And when proposing new classes and seminars, let the powers know where resource materials can be obtained for program curricula.

* * *

Letter writing needn't be an isolated action either.

There are several groups, such as IMPACT, Bread for the World, SANE, and Defenders of Wildlife that send regular information packets to their members.

These packets provide background on current issues and suggest whom to contact in each case. That makes the job of corresponding easier because they direct letters where they'll do the most good and give the writer a solid base of facts from which to work. Many groups ask to have copies of any mail sent so that they can include them in their lobbying work. Thus, the effect of a single letter is further multiplied.

Amnesty International, or A.I., a human-rights organization that works for the release of prisoners of conscience wherever they are, suggests that letter-writing meetings be held from time to time.

When members gather, they often stimulate one another to write more letters and reinforce one another as they exchange ideas and boost one another's morale. The Tucson branch of WILFP, an international peace organization, holds monthly letter-writing meetings at which writing equipment, stationery, and resources are supplied to its members and the public in general. The response to date has been gratifying. This type of action could be a real opportunity for the homebound host!

Through its Urgent Action Network, A.I. has effected the release of many prisoners. One teacher in South Africa was told by the police upon being set free that he must immediately inform A.I. of his release!

Leaders of our own country aren't the only ones susceptible to public opinion. Even those in the Soviet Union take note of their mail.

Samantha Smith was eleven when she sent her now famous letter to Brezhnev, asking him why there must be nuclear war. For whatever reason, the Soviet leader answered her letter and invited her to visit Russia as an ambassador of peace. She was allowed to speak to Soviet children in their classrooms and was permitted to spread the word that most Americans are not in favor of war with other countries. That valuable contribution resulted from a single concerned letter!

It's not necessary to write in the language of the country the letter is going to. Most foreign executive staffs have translators readily available, and it's better to say things clearly in our native tongue than to risk misusing an unfamiliar language.

The important thing is to treat the receiver with the same respect and courtesy we extend to our own leaders. Ideology and politics aren't appropriate subjects for discussion, and letters should focus on specific topics.

Most libraries can furnish the names and addresses of foreign rulers on request.

* * *

Business leaders, from corporate executives to corner-store proprietors, listen to public opinion as much as elected officials do — perhaps more so, since their sales depend on general approval.

Those who are disturbed about advertising practices, the shows a company sponsors, the quality of products on the market, or the labor or environmental practices of organizations should write to those responsible — particularly the president or chairman of the board of the offending company.

Their correspondence, of course, should follow the same rules as outlined above in being brief, to the point, courteous, and with good reasons to support their opinions. They should also challenge the business to do its best and provide, if possible, some creative solutions.

Local stores are perhaps most sensitive to customer complaint; thus, they can easily be influenced with just a few letters. But even corporations (whose addresses can be obtained through local libraries) can be swayed by remarkably few pieces of mail.

Boycotts are powerful weapons in influencing corporate policy, and letters explaining participation in a boycott are especially valuable. They reinforce the action and let a company know exactly why their sales have dipped — even if only a little. With a list of the reasons for the boycott in hand, corporate directors can steer policy in a more acceptable manner in the future, or face lost business.

* * *

Media stars, who do a great deal to mold public opinion, are also very sensitive to public pressure.

Writing to them to ask that they use their talents responsibly can often influence their career decisions. If they receive enough letters criticizing them for promoting questionable or objectionable standards, and if their studios get the same, they may be persuaded to reexamine the roles they accept.

On the other hand, personalities can use their influence to boost a variety of causes. Stars are far more politically oriented than they once were and are willing to speak out readily on issues that interest them. Robert Redford and environmental issues, Kenny Rogers and the farming crisis, and the rock group U-2 and Amnesty International immediately come to mind.

When sending letters to personalities to ask for their endorsement of an issue, we should present the facts clearly and concisely. Though they may not see the mail personally, it's often worth a try to get their support, and even a casual favorable mention from someone who's very visible can give any cause tremendous assistance.

When considering media people, too, don't overlook local celebrities, who may be much more accessible than national notables.

Radio DJ's, newspaper columnists, and TV announcers are all good bets for persuasion. Even just being able to use their names in promoting a cause often helps to "sell" a concept to a greater number of people.

But just as honey attracts more response than vinegar, positive letters are more welcome than negative ones. And they should be used as often as possible. Complimenting a TV or movie star, a company, a government official, and the like, will reinforce their good actions and give them the strength and encouragement they need to continue.

* * *

According to a survey done recently, the most-read section of any periodical is the "Letters to the Editor" column.

People enjoy reading the variety of opinions there, which are given in short, personal selections. And in many cases, a well-presented letter does change minds.

This type of letter can both be encouraging and intimidating for those who choose to write it. Encouraging, because by its nature it can influence many people instead of just one to support a cause or an issue. Intimidating, because if it is published, it forces writers to go public with their stand. Most periodicals won't publish letters without a signature, so there's no chance to remain anonymous.

There are plenty of publications that welcome letters to their editors, including local papers, regional and national magazines, and even international newspapers and periodicals. The same letter can often be sent to more than one place for maximum exposure, since different periodicals usually serve different audiences.

It's not necessary to be a subscriber to write to a particular publication, but it is essential to aim each letter at that periodical's audience, and to follow the publication's format. If at all possible, check a recent copy of the periodical in order to address its most recent concerns.

As with composing other public letters, there are a few guidelines to make letters to an editor more effective, as well as to give them a better shot at being published, which, after all, is the reason for writing them. Here are the suggested guidelines:

1. They should be kept short (about two hundred words) and deal with only one issue each.

2. Of course, they should be signed and include a return address. Many staffs like to verify correspondence, so it helps to add a phone number they can call.

3. They should be timely. If responding to an article, the sooner they're sent the better. With luck, they'll encourage others to write about the same issue and perhaps stimulate more thorough coverage of the same issues by the newspaper or magazine staff.

4. They shouldn't be too frequent. The impact of our letters can only be weakened if we write daily about any topic under the sun. If roused to an opinion only occasionally, or just on topics we've shown special expertise in, our letters will normally command respect. We may even find we've developed a following in that paper or magazine! Once a month is the best spacing for most newspapers.

"Going public" in letter writing, then, can be an exciting experience — in persuading greater numbers of people to think and act for peace and justice and to stand up for deeply held beliefs.

* * *

Formal public letters, however, aren't the only ones that help change the world. Personal correspondence is just as important and serves to benefit mankind on a very basic level.

There are plenty of lonely people — at home, in hospitals and nursing homes, away at school or in cities distant from their families and friends — whose day would be brightened considerably by a note from someone who's thinking of them. They may not seem "important" in terms of world peace or the sweeping movement of justice, but they are actually what it's all about. A just and peaceful world is one in which the people are as caring of one another as Christ Himself was.

Government social programs are often criticized because they really don't improve the "quality of life" of their participants. There simply aren't enough social workers to check on each person regularly to see that they remain cared for.

But a regular person-to-person correspondence can do what no official charity can. It can keep a person interested in and happy with life. Routine notes from someone who's really interested in an individual may help the person feel that he or she is wanted and useful. Sometimes correspondence of this type can make the difference between a person coping or "losing it" under pressure.

We can send letters to those we know personally, or to pen pals met through any number of organizations.

The International Friendship League writes to its members telling them, "You can make a friend for yourself — and for your country."

The most important thing in writing is to be faithful, and not to demand instant answers. We should be positive in tone, of course, lighthearted, understanding, and not preachy, though there's a place in most ongoing correspondence to share deeply held thoughts and convictions.

Including clippings from newspapers and magazines may sometimes enliven an otherwise routine letter, too.

* * *

International pen-pal organizations are numerous, and they do much to promote world understanding, which leads to peace.

A Soviet reporter, speaking to an American in the offices of *Pravda*, said, "We need more communication, more pen pals. It doesn't matter what they write about. They can talk about their hobbies, about anything. Maybe somehow we can bring about a change of heart."

Writers are urged to follow the above rules, and no presents should be sent to pen pals, as the duties in foreign countries are high enough to make an exchange of gifts very expensive for the receiver. But postcards, pictures, stamps, and other small items are often gratefully received.

One group suggests giving the addresses of pen pals as gifts for birthdays! It would certainly be a meaningful offering to those who are concerned about the world situation, as well as those who are lonely. Check with them first to see if they would be willing to take on regular correspondence, though.

In all types of personal correspondence, the practice of using cards, stamps, and stickers from organizations whose beliefs we hold is an exciting way to "pass the word." According to research, each piece of mail is seen by at least eight postal people, so putting a sticker on each letter increases the possibility of influencing others.

* * *

The job of working for peace and justice is often a hard and discouraging one. One way to help ease the load of those who are involved in the work is to send a note of appreciation to them, even if they're strangers.

Missionaries, pro-life workers, writers, and volunteers in the field often need the boost of a short positive note. In many cases, a news story or magazine article will mention them, and mail can reach them through writing via that periodical or the local office of their organization.

* * *

George Gaines was seventy when he began writing to the inmates of Florida's death rows. Today he and his wife send out over eight thousand pieces of mail to condemned prisoners in thirty-seven states each year! They've made quite a difference in some convicts' lives, even leading some to make peace with God before they die.

Prisoners are frequently the forgotten members of society. Shunned by their family members and former friends, they spend long, grinding days behind bars. The encouragement and friendship they need that might give them hope to begin a new life is usually denied them, and they sink deeper into pain when they're released.

Prison Fellowship, founded by former "Watergate criminal" Charles Colson, has a program that matches prisoners and outsiders through the mail. Each of the convicts chosen has given his life to Christ, and there are guidelines provided that help the correspondence to be safe and satisfactory for both sides.

There are other groups, too, that can arrange postal friendships with those in jail. A newspaper, *The Nuclear Resister*, which publishes the names and addresses of those who are imprisoned for anti-nuclear activities in the U.S., does the same for them.

* * *

Institutions such as mental hospitals and nursing homes often have residents who are forgotten and would benefit from an occasional card or letter to let them know they aren't alone. In many cases, the recipients won't be able to answer, but this is all the greater reason they'll appreciate the thought.

For those who are interested in corresponding with the residents of mental hospitals and nursing homes, an inquiry to the administration of the facility or the chaplain should bring results.

* * *

Letters are an excellent way for the homebound to practice works of mercy — visiting the sick and imprisoned, comforting the lonely, and counseling the doubtful. They can't and shouldn't be overlooked.

RESOURCES

- *Activist News Network*
  Defenders of Wildlife, 1244 Nineteenth St., N.W.,

Washington, DC 20036 (Notifies members on letter-writing projects to be undertaken that will benefit the environment with an emphasis on wildlife.)

Amnesty International U.S.A., 322 8th Ave., New York, NY 10001 (Uses letter writing for the release of the unjustly imprisoned all over the world. You must join the Urgent Action Network or Freedom Writers to participate.)

Freedom Writers, 322 8th Ave., New York, NY 10001

Urgent Action Network, P.O. Box 1270, Nederland, CO 80466

Congress Watch, 215 Pennsylvania Ave., S.E., Washington, DC 20003

International Friendship League, 55 Mt. Vernon St., Boston, MA 02108 (Matches pen pals internationally.)

IMPACT, 100 Maryland Ave., N.E., Washington, DC 20002 (Uses letter writing for lobbying various issues.)

National SANE, 711 G St., S.E., Washington, DC 20003 (Uses letter writing to lobby for nuclear policy changes.)

The Nuclear Resister, P.O. Box 1503, Ukiah, CA 95482 (Has addresses of those imprisoned for peace activities and encourages correspondence with them.)

People to People, Crown Center, 2420 Pershing Rd., Suite 300, Kansas City, MO 64108 (Matches pen pals internationally.)

Prison Fellowship, P.O. Box 11500, Washington, DC 20041 (Matches concerned Christians with prison pen pals.)

Prison Pen Pals, Box 1217, Cincinnati, OH 45202 (Matches those concerned with prison pen pals.)

- *Senators*
  The Hon. (name of senator), U.S. Senate, Washington, DC 20510

- *Representatives*
  The Hon. (name of representative), U.S. House of Representatives, Washington, DC 20515

Office of the Ambassador, Embassy of the U.S.S.R., 1125 16th St., N.W., Washington, DC 20036

Pravda Editor, ul. Prardy 24, Moscow, A-47, 125867 GSP, U.S.S.R.

New York Times "Letters to the Editor," 229 W. 43rd St., New York, NY 10036

Chicago Tribune "Letters to the Editor," 435 N. Michigan Ave., Chicago, IL 60611

Washington Post "Letters to the Editor," 1150 15th St., N.W., Washington, DC 20071

Newsweek "Letters to the Editor," 444 Madison Ave., New York, NY 10022

Time "Letters to the Editor," Time-Life Bldg., Rockefeller Center, New York, NY 10020

Common Cause, 2030 M St., N.W., Washington, DC 20036

Greenpeace U.S.A., 1611 Connecticut Ave., N.W., Washington, DC 20009 (Has activist networks for wildlife, toxics, and disarmament questions.)

5
other writing

    Correspondence is just the beginning when it comes to writing for the benefit of the world, though.

    The options are endless for those who find they enjoy writing and have some workable talent. They can try penning books, scripts, articles, newsletters, pamphlets, and brochures, as well as ads and other throwaways.

* * *

    Authoring a book is a job that intimidates most people. Yet for those who try, the rewards of producing a stimulating and well-done volume can be almost overwhelming.

Even those with little experience can, with sincere effort, often turn out creditable works. With equal parts of information, technique, and sweat, they can learn to put together volumes that will stir the public to act for the good of all.

Harriet Beecher Stowe felt so strongly about slavery and the abolition movement of her time that she was moved to write a short novel, *Uncle Tom's Cabin*. It shook the American people.

Abraham Lincoln recognized her contribution and once greeted her with, "So you're the little lady who started this big war." A left-handed compliment, surely, but a tribute to the power of her written words.

Even in today's electronic media society, writing is a powerful force. It started the ecology movement (*Silent Spring* by Rachel Carson), sparked the consumer cause (*Unsafe at Any Speed* by Ralph Nader), and stirred compassion for blacks during the civil-rights movement (*Black Like Me* by John Griffin). And fiction is as important in creating an atmosphere of acceptance for an idea as is nonfiction.

Books need not be published by large houses in order to get a message to the public. There are many small specialized publishers who are very approachable and who will consider works on peace and justice topics. They usually have a good market established for these works, and they're often in a position to help new authors of promise with individual attention. Checking current books in our field of interest will usually turn up the names of receptive publishers.

There's also the option of self-publishing, in which a

writer prepares his final text, lines up a printer, and sells his work himself. Paying for all of this can be fairly expensive, but many authors find they're willing to foot the bill in order to get their message as they want it to the public.

Henry David Thoreau wrote and published his masterwork, *Walden*, by himself. When he was asked one time about the size of his library, he answered, "I have hundreds of volumes in my house — and most of them are *Walden!*"

Self-published books can be registered and copyrighted with the Library of Congress (though it's not required), but the authors needn't file their activities with the state. Thus, paperwork is minimal, which can definitely be an incentive to those who want to write and be heard.

* * *

Movies, television, and the theater all cry for good playwrights who can get a message across dramatically. Their influence has been well established both by observation and academic studies.

The movie *Gandhi* aroused a great deal of interest in the twentieth century's foremost proponent of nonviolence. After its great success, there was a marked increase in the sale of the Mahatma's works, and renewed experiments in using his ideas.

Then we have the TV special *The Day After*, which was outstanding in its portrayal of the devastation of nuclear attack. It inspired much comment and discussion, leading to some significant citizen actions against the nuclear buildup.

Though playwriting takes years to perfect, it's a field that talented writers can't afford to ignore as they search for ways to motivate the public to grow in wisdom and compassion.

One way of becoming proficient in this talent is to write for a small group of friends and have them read the parts. As the piece takes coherent shape, and even becomes presentable, someone can videotape the group and offer the tape to a local public-access channel on TV. The play can also be done for church groups, schools, and organizations.

A variation of script-writing is composing sermons. Although most clergy prefer to write their own, they may be open to having a homily submitted for a special occasion. The best way to get a response is to send a sample of a sermon to clergymen you have contacted, along with the offer of more.

* * *

From the time of the American radicals' *Journal of Public Occurrences*, which fanned extensive anti-British sentiment in colonial times, newspaper and magazine columnists in the United States have exerted great power on public attitudes. The influence has been regularly used and abused, too, from Hearst's "yellow journalism" that started the Spanish-American War to the effective muckraking journalism typified by Bernstein and Woodward during Watergate.

Today, it's important to use that power responsibly for the good of all.

In 1985, there were 20,572 magazines and newspapers being published in the United States alone. Of those, a large percentage actively solicited manuscripts from writers who could inform, entertain, or inspire their readers.

So the field is open for those at home who feel they can write and are willing to put time and effort into getting their message out to the general public through the printed media. A good place to break in is on the Op Ed (opposite editorial) pages of various newspapers. The next step up from letters to the editor, they contain short opinion pieces on topics of general public interest.

As writers build up reputation and skill, they'll find they're able to sway a large number of people and perhaps bring about some much needed reforms.

But self-publishing is possible here, too.

Dorothea Monteith, a seventy-six-old Canadian woman, who's confined to a wheelchair herself, puts out a monthly newsletter for shut-ins and those who are institutionalized. It's her effort to encourage and sustain them, and, according to the "Christopher Newsnotes," she's said, "I feel the Lord has permitted me to be a shut-in for His glory."

Newsletters such as hers are used for a variety of reasons and are very flexible in scope for most writers. Those who've tried the medium have found that:

√ They can be produced by an individual or a group.

√ They can be mimeographed, photocopied, run off quickly on a computer printer, or be set up elaborately with graphics at a professional printing firm.

√ They can address the general public, or be targeted to a specific audience.

√ They can be any length, and of any frequency.

✓They can be distributed in the mail or on the street.

In any case, they are a fine, unfettered way to affect readers on a regular basis.

Churches, organizations, and causes often need someone to serve as a clearinghouse for information and they welcome volunteers for the job. Running a newsletter for these groups is satisfying and helps solve both the problem of input and of audience.

Because it's not necessary to copyright the material in a newsletter, or to register it with anyone, this option remains an open and viable choice for all.

* * *

At every street fair, convention, rally, and concert-with-a-cause, there are stacks of brochures and pamphlets given away: "Portrait of a Peacemaker"; "Your Telephone Taxes Pay for War"; "Acid Rain — The Invisible Threat." The titles go on and on, and the information they spread is invaluable.

Someone has to write all of that material — and that person could be a homebound author.

Often, groups will have their own staff write their material so that they can control content and style more easily. But if an individual presents them with a concrete idea, or outline for a pamphlet, they'll often respond enthusiastically.

Just as with Thomas Paine's *Common Sense*, brochures and pamphlets can be individually produced, too. They require a knowledge of graphics and printing, but doing the job solo allows a lot of latitude and assures that the piece ends up as the author intended it to.

Even if a brochure is written without the specific

backing of a group, most organizations are more than happy to supply any research material needed, as well as production advice if they are able.

* * *

A final suggestion for those who want to try their hand at public writing, but don't feel they have the stamina or talent for long pieces, is to advertise.

Advertisements aren't the exclusive right of Madison Avenue, and they can be used for much more than just hawking products.

Slogans have been used for years to sell ideas, such as "Only YOU can prevent forest fires" and "Give until it helps." Whether they appear on billboards or in small spaces in the backs of magazines, they filter into the public consciousness and *do* make a difference in the way people think.

Some ads are large and attention-getting, going far beyond the slogan category.

After the U.S. attack on Libya, concerned members of Beyond War, a peace organization, took out a full-page ad in the *Los Angeles Times* to put forward the idea that military actions weren't the only way to solve problems between nations. They included the address of the local Beyond War chapter, and had a gratifying response from many who were looking for a way to counteract what they felt was useless action.

And in 1949, when the Cold War was just beginning, a full-page ad was run in the *New York Times* by concerned men who urged that people turn to prayer. The result was the formation of today's Fellowship in Prayer.

Because many organizations are chronically short of

funds, the practice of placing ads in papers to announce their activities is a great way to assist them. After checking essential facts as to time, place, and circumstances, any individual can compose an ad that, when run, will increase the event's visibility. Even one well-placed notice can increase public interest by a significant amount. It may mean the difference between a successful event and a "disappointing turnout."

Advertising can be fun and in most cases is very effective in stirring up the public. It doesn't take a great deal of time to put a public notice together, and the results are often far beyond the expected.

* * *

Using the pen for worthy causes is an honorable and critical profession. It can be done at home, in privacy, and has a definite impact on the life of the world. It's both public and private, combining the best features of each.

6
using the phone

"I never really understood what a telephone was for until I watched the bishop in action," marveled his assistant.

When Bishop Floyd Begin was the ordinary of Oakland, California, he found that because he was stationed in a crowded, decaying area, it was impossible to make personal visits to his flock, who were much in need of attention. So within a short time after his appointment there, he developed a schedule of phone calling to get his work done — and was so successful that many said he was able to accomplish twice as much as a regular parish priest.

Chatting with those who were lonely or in trouble, networking for those who needed help, and in general just keeping in touch with those he was responsible for kept him busy on the telephone for hours each day. His parishioners felt cared for and special when the bishop called. As a result, these feelings stimulated them to be faithful in their Church's life.

The same ministry can be carried on in various ways today by both clergy and laity, and is especially relevant for those who are homebound.

Telephones are communication devices — nothing more nor less. Although many people fear, dread, or just dislike using them because of their impersonality, phones have been instruments of peace, used for every purpose — from making lonely people's lives more bearable to swinging key votes in Congress. The art is in knowing how and when to use them.

When are phones most effectively used?

Whenever immediate personal contact is necessary, or when time is a critical factor in communication.

The general rules of politeness, of course, apply to any use of the telephone. Speaking clearly, courteously, and briefly is most important. Listening is just as important as talking, so we should provide plenty of opportunity for response.

In political calls, it's essential to assure that the person to whom we're talking is the one we want to reach. Having to repeat a message, especially more than once, tends to dilute enthusiasm and weaken our final effect.

* * *

Phones, like letters, are very effective when they're used in the public arena.

Most government representatives have local numbers in their districts to serve their constituents. Phoning them with opinions, especially immediately before controversial votes, can influence many who are undecided. Each call is reckoned as representing fifty voters, according to their staffs, and it's respected accordingly.

Even the White House has a telephone number for public remarks. Those who phone (202) 456-7639 will reach the Comment Section, and the operator on duty will answer, "The Executive Offices of the President." She (or he) will then take any messages and relay them to the appropriate party from the president on down.

Telegrams are closely linked to phone calls in their uses and effects, except that legislators are more impressed by them, as they get so few. Their staffs count each telegram as representing two hundred fifty voters!

Western Union has an Opiniongram service that they'll bill to a home phone number. Twenty words cost five dollars and will reach the person it's sent to within twenty-four hours. The number is (800) 332-6000.

"Telephone trees" are very efficient and are an integral practice of popular lobbying groups. (Bread for the World, SANE, and IMPACT are prime employers of this type of communication.) In them, a central contact in Washington calls a local member about an issue that needs quick lobbying pressure. That member then passes on the message to those assigned to him. They, in turn, call others on their "branch," and so on. All of these people are then expected to communicate with their member of Congress, or whomever else is affected, on that particular topic.

The idea can be used on a local and statewide level, too. It might even be used by the members of a church group to respond to certain types of problems, such as objectionable TV programs or local tragedies. As a result, stations could be deluged with calls by irate viewers after an offensive ad or program is shown, or a network of support might be arranged through police or fire departments for the victims of a disaster.

Those who are homebound are ideal as coordinators or facilitators of phone trees because of their general availability.

In addition to lobbying legislators, phone trees are an effective way to get people to participate in significant events. Reminding those interested the night before that a rally or demonstration is coming up is valuable in "getting out the troops." Hastily-called actions also need to be publicized through the use of phone trees to maximize their effect.

Phone trees can be formal or informal, extensive or limited — but the greater the number of participants, the more powerful a "tree" is. Therefore, telephone trees should be a primary option in the consideration of one who's looking for a way to help advance a particular cause.

Two projects closely related to phone trees can be carried out by home-based persons for the cause they're most interested in. They're the telephone survey and the hot line.

Many groups, both local and national, need some sort

of input on various issues that concern them, and one of the best ways to get the views of the public at large is through the use of telephone surveys. Finding people who will spend time calling others, though, is especially difficult if the groups can't afford to pay for their services. Usually, callers set their own hours and sometimes tabulate results before sending them in.

Those who are searching for a way to serve from home can notify these groups to make them aware that they're available for action. Occasionally, a survey call will result in interesting conversation and turn into an educational experience for both parties.

Sometimes organizations have never thought of doing a phone survey. If this is the case, a well thought-out set of survey questions with objectives plainly stated may encourage them to try the effort. The fact should be stressed for those who haven't used the technique before that just by conducting a survey, more people will become familiar with the name and aims of a group. Planning a survey can be exciting and rewarding, especially as the results come in.

Surveys should be conducted under the auspices of an established group, of course, as the method has been abused, and many people are leery of answering questions from callers who are not affiliated with well-known groups.

Hot lines are another intriguing project for those who are interested.

These lines are used for answering questions as well as for referring those with problems or with information to the proper people. They require one who's well versed in that field (again, education is very important!) and who has patience and the ability to communicate well.

Though hot-line phones are usually based in a central location so that they can be manned around the clock, small groups will occasionally have a member who will field calls from his or her home.

It's fairly expensive to set up a hot line and list it in the telephone book. So if a group wants it to be publicized that way, the group should be willing to shoulder the cost itself. The benefits to the group and to the public are invaluable.

* * *

Invalids often need friends who will check on them daily to see how they're doing. As a matter of fact, many people have been able to remain independent only because of such regular contact with others.

Routine callers are as important to one whose autonomy is shaky as are visiting nurses and social workers. The person calling can be either a personal friend or a volunteer who's been put in touch with the invalid through a service bureau.

Mentally retarded citizens are also, in some areas, paired with phone liaisons. They can share their day-to-day hopes and joys with them or discuss their problems in coping with an often confusing world.

Since de-institutionalization has been the rule, more and more retarded are required to live in the community, and there is a great need for those who are willing to show them the interest and compassion they need to continue. Although some training is usually required for this type of phone work, it can usually be obtained through a volunteer service bureau.

No matter what the level of communication, though, it serves to ease the anxiety that goes with unsupervised living.

The concern that most of us feel in calling a stranger is understandable. We're not sure what to say, or if what we say will be interpreted properly. This is where the attitude of trust comes in.

* * *

Jesus may not have been referring to phone ministry when He said, ". . . Do not be anxious how you are to speak or what you are to say; for what you are to say will be given to you in that hour. . ." (Matthew 10:19). But His words can offer a great deal of comfort as we dial a new person's number.

Trying to see others as we do ourselves helps us to shed our self-consciousness, too. Though at first we may want to make a few notes to help us over the rough spots, conversations become more natural as time goes on. We'll find that much of the time our input is less important than our listening. That, after all, is the most important part of a phone minister's work.

One idea that a few individuals have tried is that of establishing a "listening line." It requires patience and the willingness to give up privacy. But for those who are called to total dedication — publishing their phone numbers in a parish bulletin as individuals who are available to listen, pray, and chat with those who need it — the option is a worthy one.

The marshall of one small Arizona town tried the

concept with local high-school students who were running wild. He addressed them at a school assembly, and offered them his phone number to be used at night, if they felt they needed help. His offer was occasionally abused, as he expected it would be; but on the whole, it was an encouraging success. The teenagers respected him, and the disturbance rate was significantly lowered.

* * *

Bishop Nicolas E. Walsh once told the story of some members of a college fraternity who were fed up with the "trash rock" they were hearing on their favorite radio station. After stewing about what they, as individuals, could do about it, they decided to call the station and protest the worst of the songs as they were played.

They did, and told the disc jockey they'd appreciate a change. They reminded him that they generally supported his sponsors and bought many records. He discussed the matter with his station manager who called them back in ten minutes. He said he wholeheartedly agreed with them about the offensive songs and was cutting them from his program!

The job of registering complaints (or kudos) as they're earned is an interesting one. It can bring satisfying rewards as the above, or frustrating indifference. But letting a radio manager know that his station is being heard by calling immediately after the stimulus is broadcast, makes him more receptive to each suggestion.

Although many stations have only "canned" (prerecorded) news, others are very open to listener participation. It's possible to call in "hot" news, or information directly relevant to the day's stories, and get it on the air the same day. It's best to prepare a statement ahead of time, keeping it short (one word = one second) and fact-filled. It's very likely that a caller with good, pertinent information will be interviewed on the phone immediately, and that interview will be used on the next broadcast.

Then there are the radio talk shows, which beg for participants.

These shows depend for their lives on wide response, so they welcome controversial calls. Most serve an ample and loyal audience, too. That's why it's worthwhile to monitor them and offer opinions as the opportunities arise.

To cover the talk show possibilities most effectively, it's helpful to have near the phone a list of the shows, their times, station numbers, phone numbers, and the names of the hosts. Organized information and clippings should also be kept handy for reference and backup. Moreover, the shows should be monitored regularly to get the flavor of how they're run.

People who partake in the dialog on these shows are just ordinary individuals, without broadcast training or special experience in the media. Many of them "make the rounds" of local stations, calling first one, then another, to spread their ideas over the widest possible area. And many of them are effective in changing minds. Remembering this, no one needs to feel self-conscious or intimidated by having others hear him or her talk. Adding a word for the rights of the unborn or a nuclear freeze can only help to stimulate thought and create an open atmosphere.

A well thought-out presentation may introduce an issue to someone who's unfamiliar with it, or change someone's mind on a current topic.

* * *

Computer networks are the "new kids on the block" in the field of communications, but they're becoming more common and, therefore, many of them have services specifically geared to the needs of those in the peace movement.

Through the use of these computer links, which are transmitted over phone lines, people from all over the world can share information and ideas; they can also build up grass-roots action and support groups.

Networks function either by "conferencing," which allows many users to communicate during a single time frame, or through the use of "billboards." This last allows people to enter messages on a particular topic at any time. Others with access to the billboard can tap into the system to respond or pick up whatever information is interesting to them.

* * *

From making private calls to check up on another's welfare to basking in the fleeting fame that results from participating in a late-night talk show, telephone callers have a wide opportunity to serve God and mankind from home.

RESOURCES

Bread for the World, 802 Rhode Island Ave., N.E.,

Washington, DC 20018 (Has a quick-line telephone lobbying program.)

Econet Computer Network, 15290 Cleman Valley Rd., Occidental, CA 95465 (An international ecological telecommunications network.)

National SANE, 711 G St., S.E., Washington, DC 20003 (Has a rapid-response telephone lobbying program.)

PeaceNet Computer Link, 1918 Bonita, Berkeley, CA 94704

7
hospitality

"Welcome one another, therefore, as Christ has welcomed you, for the glory of God" (Romans 15:7).

One talent many people overlook when they evaluate their aptitudes is that of hospitality.

The gifts of making others feel at home and wanted, of really listening to them, and of sending them on their way refreshed and renewed are just as important in creating a peaceful and just world as are writing letters and books, phoning members of Congress, or organizing demonstrations.

Mother Teresa calls the poverty of the affluent Western nations the worst in the world because it involves crushing loneliness, the "hunger for love, for care, to be somebody to someone," and the "homelessness that comes from having no one to call your own."

Those who genuinely open themselves and their homes to others, even on a casual basis, are helping to transform the bleak impersonal world so prevalent today into a warm and caring society.

Most opportunities for this kind of ministry are informal and spontaneous. We may casually mention to neighbors and friends that they're always welcome to come in and chat, to share a cup of tea, or that we have an extra bed in case they need one for a house overflowing with guests. Sometimes listening politely and calmly to a salesman or door-to-door canvasser may be all such a person needs to cope with an otherwise frustrating day.

As the author Madeleine L'Engle says, "As long as anyone cares, it is an icon of God's caring."

But there are more systematic ways of being hospitable, too.

One way is to let a local college or university know that we're available to "adopt" a student. First-year scholars are often lonely and could use an anchor — a substitute mother or grandparent they can just come to sit with and visit.

At St. Mary of the Plains College in Dodge City, Kansas, local alumni of the school adopt homesick kids and help them cope with the problems of their new environment. They try to be available when needed and often build long-lasting relationships with a variety of students.

Schools are usually happy to refer their students to those who volunteer. There are some guidelines to follow for best results on both sides (such as not getting financially involved with one another), but the rewards can be outstanding and may sometimes make the difference between a student being able to remain in school and having to drop out.

In large cities, there are often families of seriously ill patients who need to be near them, but who live far away. Hotel and motel bills are often beyond their means, and many find themselves sleeping in waiting rooms and lobbies at the hospital. They get no respite from the hospital atmosphere at a time when they most need it to keep their spirits up.

Though there are Ronald MacDonald Houses in many cities where the parents of terminally ill children can stay, even they are sometimes overcrowded.

A very useful option, then, is to contact the volunteer office at a local hospital and offer the use of a spare room or couch for a night or two at a time to those who need it. Even if their only real needs are a shower and a cup of coffee in a private setting, the family members will appreciate the chance to be away from the hospital for a time.

Victims of fires and other disasters often need temporary shelter, too. Letting the St. Vincent de Paul Society, Red Cross office, or local Victim/Witness Assistance

Project people know of your offer is an effective way of being available.

Holidays are lonely times for many people, and dinners eaten alone are especially depressing. So offering to host one or two others for a festive meal is a great way to feed the hungry, comfort the lonely, and have a special feast all at the same time. Church bulletins and Newman Centers are fine places to advertise for guests, while contacting social service bureaus will also usually turn up a wealth of those who need some cheer.

* * *

There are several groups that foster international hospitality. By matching hosts and travelers, they promote world peace. Because they believe the key to understanding is in personal contact between private citizens, they facilitate home stays among their members.

Servas and People to People are two of these organizations. They encourage making private homes available for the stay of a few nights to voyagers to forge friendships and understanding among those of different nations.

Servas also accepts those who just want to spend an afternoon with a traveler, sharing ideas and experiences over a hot cup of tea.

The entertainment group Up With People also seeks homes for their people to stay in for short periods of time. The group's members usually need only a place to sleep, as they're busy most of the day with rehearsals and such, but the time spent together can be an exciting learning experience for both hosts and performers.

For those who are willing to commit themselves to

long-term hospitality, hosting a foreign exchange student is always a fascinating option. Through allowing a student to live at one's home for a year, the host is making real the motto of the International Youth Exchange: "Help bring the world together one friendship at a time."

Dwight D. Eisenhower, thirty-fourth U.S. president, clearly saw the possibilities of people-to-people exchanges in the role of promoting world peace. "If we are going to take advantage of the assumption that all people want peace," he said, "then the problem is for people to get together and to leap governments . . . to work out not one method, but thousands of methods by which people can gradually learn a little bit more of each other."

Long-term hospitality can be used in other ways, too.

Some of those concerned with the abortion question can offer pregnant women without resources a place to stay during their pregnancy. It presents a real and immediate choice and can be arranged through pro-life organizations such as Birthright.

A California woman offers an interesting variation of this idea. She takes in the babies of women who are in a nearby jail and cares for them as if they were her own. She also arranges to bring them to their moms on a regular basis so that the family ties aren't lost.

Another way to practice hospitality for the benefit of all is to volunteer to regularly host meetings for Renew, prayer groups, Alcoholics Anonymous meetings, or small organizations devoted to peace and justice. Often, the use of a regular gathering place will stimulate a new group to grow and be fruitful. The problems of where to gather each month or how to come up with funds to rent a meeting place are solved, and that allows members to concentrate their energies and funds on their real concerns.

Even just making a space available for occasional forums, movies, retreats, or parties is invaluable to beginning organizations.

* * *

Listening is a major part of hospitality. In many cases, those who come seeking comfort at the kitchen table just need a chance to vent their concerns or problems. Providing an attentive ear and quiet atmosphere is an excellent way of ministering to them. Martin E. Marty calls the practice of sympathetic listening the "sacrament of the coffeepot."

Roger Schutz, the abbot of Taizé, who has a well-known ministry among young people in Europe, contends that the most important thing he does for them is to listen. He doesn't see himself as an important teacher but as one who makes himself available to others, through whom they can eventually find their way. And his work has been very fruitful.

A special kind of listening is also a recognized peace technique. It requires some training, though no college degree is necessary and it can be used on any level, from the personal to the international.

It's called mediation.

Trained mediators are often called upon to facilitate dispute settlements (the most common are those between labor and management). Though it's not technically necessary to have certification to mediate, it is recommended that a course in technique be taken. Many facilities will accept only trained mediators.

Mediators are usually presented with the facts from both sides of an argument, and arrange meetings with the antagonists — providing a nonthreatening atmosphere in which problems can be hammered out. Though each side usually agrees to abide by the results of the mediation session, sometimes both sides will use them merely as jumping-off points for further negotiations.

Mediators can be either paid or not, and, depending on the problem, a case may take anywhere from a matter of hours to several months. Being a mediator, moreover, takes a great deal of patience, sensitivity, and a strong sense of justice.

Once a person is trained and ready, he or she may register with a parish or civic counsel as being available to help out in this way.

* * *

The old-fashioned virtue of neighborliness is closely related to hospitality.

Accepting packages and deliveries for those who aren't home, doing short-term baby-sitting or caring for pets in emergencies, and even taking calls occasionally for those who are without a phone are ways of showing those who live near us that we care. It builds a bond between neighbors. Moreover, it creates the kind of trust and cooperation that are necessary for building a just world.

In the past few years, a program called "Neighborhood Watch" has gained momentum in many cities. Those who live in an area agree to stay alert to what's going on there. If unusual activity occurs, or there seems to be some trouble, those in the program notify the proper authorities for more investigation. The system leads to safer and more responsive places to live.

* * *

Christ praised the hospitality of Mary, Martha, and Lazarus and loved to rest at their home. Their example of welcoming Christ in their family is an inspiring one and can serve as a pattern for the actions of many homebound.

RESOURCES

U.S. Servas Committee, Inc., 11 John St., New York, NY 10038

People to People, Crown Center, 2420 Pershing Rd., Suite 300, Kansas City, MO 64108

- *Mediation*
  Ongoing programs include:

  San Francisco Community Boards, San Francisco, Calif.

  Mediation Services, Stamford, Conn.

  Neighborhood Justice Center of Atlanta, Atlanta, Ga.

  Christian Conciliation Service, Oak Park, Ill.

  Children's Hearings Project, Cambridge, Mass.

  Center for Dispute Settlement, Rochester, N.Y.

  Columbus Night Prosecutor Program, Columbus, Ohio

Community Association for Mediation, Pittsburgh, Pa.

Washington Arbitration Service, Seattle, Wash.

(The Education Section of the Seattle, Wash., Public Library has a dispute-resolution program with full bibliographies.)

8
other talents

Charisms come in many colors.

All are important, and each complements the others to create a just and whole world.

St. Paul recognized this diversity of talents when he wrote to the Ephesians that some of the Holy Spirit's gifts to Christians "were that some should be apostles, some prophets, some evangelists, some pastors and teachers, for the equipment of the saints, for building up the body of Christ" (Ephesians 4:11-12).

No one can feed the hungry without the help of those

who raise the food. No one can teach without the background that comes from reading the works of writers who have gone before. And those who clothe the naked can't do that without the work of seamstresses and tailors.

The important fact is that we use our talents to the best of our ability for God and man.

In this chapter, we'll explore some diverse talents and see how they can be used in "building up the body of Christ."

ART • Through the ages, many artists have used their talents to inspire the public with understanding and compassion.

The craftsmen and sculptors of Chartres cathedral in France designed their works to instruct the illiterate in the stories of the Bible. Hogarth's series of paintings, which he called "mute morality plays," spurred social reform in eighteenth-century England. And icon makers of the Middle East and Russia have long created beautiful helps to prayer and meditation with their images of God and the saints.

Today, artists who are homebound are in no way hampered in this type of creativity. No matter what medium they work in, they can use it to produce stirring art that will touch people's minds and hearts, inspiring them to action or meditation.

Getting their works shown is possible, too. Homebound artists have nearly as much access to galleries and publishers as their mobile counterparts, and they can arrange for showings of their work through agents or by mail, using slides of their creations. In some cases, artists will find immense encouragement and support in other members of a cause they espouse.

Art includes more than painting on canvas or working in clay, though. It also encompasses the commercial field. And that can be very rewarding in terms of "useful art."

Brochures, pamphlets, and books all cry for graphics that will entice browsers to read their contents, and the more professional looking they are, the better. In fact, writers often need illustrators to make their works more appealing or complete.

An artist who is committed to a particular issue, and educated in it, will often create more meaningful work than someone who is technically good, but has no feel for the questions at hand.

Home-based artists can operate as other free-lancers do in this area, by contacting groups and publishers with samples of their work and letting them know they're available for assignments.

Posters and signs are a vital part of any movement. They provide color and convey ideas succinctly. They can also become symbols for an entire crusade. Plastered on a brick wall, or stapled to the crossbar of a marcher's sign, they speak to passersby instantly and powerfully. Unusual signs at public events quite often become focal points for news cameras' coverage.

Sister Corita was a West Coast teaching nun at the time she created her simple poster, "War is not healthy for children and other living things." Her design was eventually used on a wide scale during the Vietnam conflict and helped change the consciousness of an entire country.

Silk-screening is also an effective way of spreading any message. Because it can be used for quality posters, T-shirts, and other media that must be reproduced many times, it's a form of popular art especially suited to the needs of a cause.

Logos or symbols are essential to any organization. The pro-life rose and the peace movement's dove, for example, are immediately recognizable. A challenge for the dedicated artist, logos or symbols convey the image of a group at a glance. They serve to unify those who work for the cause, and make them feel part of a viable community. When a group is formed, a good designer might offer to create a logo for its members, perhaps by submitting a selection of drawings for their choice.

Posters and other graphics, too, can be submitted on an optional basis to a group. In most cases, the work will be gratefully received and used, especially if it's offered just before a special event. Many marchers and people who attend rallies don't have the time to make their own signs, and they're happy to carry meaningful, home-produced placards.

Another artistic talent that can be used effectively is that of cartooning. From Thomas Nast to Garry B. Trudeau, cartoonists have exerted a great deal of influence on the collective mind of the American people. Nast's cartoons even led to the downfall of corrupt Tammany Hall in nineteenth-century New York City. Today, those skilled in the medium can use it just as effectively, though it may take some time to build up a loyal audience.

One way to begin is to send in samples of work to specialized magazines and newspapers that agree with the cartoonists' general outlook. From there, the more popular press may pick up a strip, thus giving it a wider audience and letting it reach the man in the street.

CRAFTS • Crafts really came into their own in the U.S. in the early seventies, when the general public grew weary of mass-produced "stuff" and people tried making personalized quality items. The term, always loose, came to include everything from silversmithing to pottery throwing to stitching lovely, lofty quilts. They somehow seemed to be related to a sane and whole life.

Handworked items are still popular, though fewer people are making them. And they can be used to support a variety of causes.

Perhaps crafts' primary value to activist groups is their ability to bring in needed funds. They may be auctioned or raffled off. Or they may be sold outright.

In any case, items are most valuable if they in some way promote the message of the cause that's marketing them. Well-balanced terrariums for environmentalist groups, kitchen plaques with prayers of thanksgiving for hunger action associations, or lovable rag dolls for child-abuse organizations are good examples of meaningful crafts.

One popular craft project over the years has been the making of quilts. They're usually produced by several people, working together or separately, and have been used for a variety of purposes. Some individuals and groups have made small quilts for pro-life organizations to give to prospective mothers. And U.S.-U.S.S.R. "Friendship Quilts" have been exchanged between various cities of these nations to promote brotherhood. Projects like these build up community both among those who make them and those who receive them.

Other types of sewing can be done for the direct benefit of the poor, too.

The tradition of sewing for the poor is old and honorable, and in the New Testament a widow named Dorcas was remembered for this type of generosity. Acts 9:39 tells us that when Peter arrived at her funeral, "All the widows stood beside him weeping, and showing coats and garments which Dorcas made while she was with them." After praying, Peter raised Dorcas from the dead.

Today, making clothes and household items for the needy is just as important as it was in Dorcas's time. Donating baby clothes to pro-life counseling centers, sewing warm winter clothes for those at shelters for the homeless, repairing linen for small clinics, etc., can be invaluable in promoting the cause of social justice.

Home-produced banners are usually welcomed by churches to spark the liturgy. They can be made in a variety of styles, from the elaborate "Lady of Guadalupe" types to simple felt ones that add so much to modern worship. Designing one, then donating it to a parish church, can be an exciting and interesting experience.

Making games and toys for children that stress cooperation and strong values is another much needed craft. They're an alternative to the competitive and questionable toys marketed by the commercial trade and will be cherished by those who receive them.

TAPING • It hardly seems possible that the ability to read could be used for more than private pleasure, but it's actually a very valuable skill for activists.

Reading for the visually impaired, the illiterate, and those who because of illness or other reasons are unable to read for themselves is a satisfying way to enrich their lives.

"Sunsounds" is a group based in Tucson, Arizona, that serves just this audience. According to their studio manager, members of the "Sunsounds" serve the blind, the dyslexic, the palsied, those with severe arthritis, and others by reading from newspapers, books, and magazines on a special radio station. "Sunsounds" is one of a network of stations in almost every state of the U.S. that does this, and most of its readers are unpaid volunteers. Although readers usually come into the studio, the homebound are welcome, and, once their work has been approved, they can submit cassette tapes to the station for airplay.

The same concept can be used to help individuals, too. One person can tape material for others on a regular basis, keeping them up-to-date on the news, or just adding to their enjoyment by reading interesting, instructive, or specially requested books. Tapes can be reused often, which makes the project inexpensive to keep up, as the main cost is in time and effort.

Activists in various fields often don't have time to read much; so taping literature from their specific areas of interest is a boon for them. They can play it on their car stereos, or during convenient times at home.

Newsnotes from the "Sierra Defense Fund Newsletter" and "Defenders of Wildlife Activist News" might be appreciated by an environmentalist, for example, just as articles from *Fellowship* (the magazine of the Fellowship of Reconciliation) or the Catholic Worker Movement's *Catholic Worker* could benefit a peace activist. This service is probably best arranged by offering it to busy or handicapped friends.

In George Gaines's "Life Row" letter-writing ministry, he and his wife often use audiotapes to send messages and music to their correspondents. It serves as a treat for men and women serving life sentences in prison and brings them a little loving contact.

For those willing to tackle the project, making tapes for radio play is another outlet.

Many cities have community radio stations whose program directors are quite open to receiving material from the public. They review tapes as they receive them, and if they pass standards, chances are good they'll be scheduled at some time during the day — though perhaps not during prime time.

Some stations are even amenable to running a series or a new program, if it's good, fits the format, and can be sustained. Each station has its own criteria, and contacting the station manager with a proposal is the best way to find out what those criteria are.

Even commercial stations are open to opinion spots and public rebuffs of their editorials. According to Federal law, they must supply equal time within twenty-four hours for those who dissent from their views. Chances are excellent of being taped while reading a prepared statement over the phone, or of having a home-recorded tape played if it's solicited first. Again, the station manager would be the one to clear the broadcast.

UPI and AP, two of the world's largest news services, both have audio networks that accept locally produced tapes for possible airplay by their affiliates. Requests and suggestions can be made to their local news desks, and short tapes of good quality can be forwarded to them. They should be bright and interesting, with some sound effects in addition to the human voice included for the best chance of getting them aired.

* * *

Videotapes are a natural extension of audiotaping.

The techniques of videotaping are, of course, different from those of audio, but for people with an artistic bent, they're soon mastered and can be invaluable in getting across vital messages. It's not necessary to have a full-scale studio to produce them either, but VCR equipment must be used.

A quiet place with appropriate props can be as effective as a commercial set in many cases. Book reading, fireside chats, and detailed instructions or presentations on any topic are possible, and they *can* be broadcast!

Public-access stations accept homemade videos, as long as they don't violate FCC regulations. These stations are required to air videos for free, though again not necessarily during prime time, and the audience must have cable TV to receive their programs.

But you don't have to rely exclusively on television stations to broadcast your videotapes. Activist groups are often interested in showing films for their members. Individual classes at schools are frequently glad to get good tapes that pertain to their subject — especially if they're free. Even church groups have a place for showing well thought-out programs on various topics. The key to effective distribution is to contact groups, and make sure you give a good description of what the tape is about.

After videos have been broadcast or used by the groups or classes they were intended for, they can be donated to public or private libraries. Because videotapes are relatively new, many libraries are more than happy to build up their collections through donations, and that ensures a larger audience for each copy. Organizations also welcome more resources for their members.

TEACHING • Many people have a knack for teaching and like to do it. The lack of a university degree or the fact that they can't get out of their houses often stops them from using their talents, though.

It shouldn't.

There's no reason why small seminars can't be held occasionally or even regularly in private homes. As a matter of fact, many people learn most effectively in just such a setting, and the idea exchange at a well-run seminar is exciting and stimulating. Any subject matter is fair game for private classes and study groups.

The free universities that flourished in the late sixties and early seventies were based on the concept that those who have something to teach and those who want to learn shouldn't have to go through a formal institution to get together. (Schools tend to filter what can be taught and how it should be done. And many believe that the free exchange of information is too important to be left to this filtering process.)

Author Richard Foster writes, "Give someone a PhD, a professorship, and he . . . will be able to teach! But . . . the position does not guarantee that the power is there."

Peter Maurin, the co-founder of the Catholic Worker Movement, felt that an essential part of his program for change was the establishment of round-table discussions for the "clarification of thought." Private home seminars are a good way of carrying out that idea, and they can be aimed at stimulating ideas and applications on topics not usually covered by normal teaching institutions. Discussing the bishops' pastoral letters, new teachings in the fields of social justice, current events from a Christian point of view, and the like, can be exciting, and is certainly valuable. It even carries out Maurin's expressed ideal for the Catholic Worker Movement — "To make the encyclicals click."

Teaching was recognized as a peacemaking technique by Pope John Paul II in 1982 when he said, "Those who, by providing information, remove the barrier of distance, so that we feel truly concerned at the fate of faraway men and women who are victims of war or injustice, are working for peace."

Advertising is very important in reaching students. Specialized newsletters, bulletins, and magazines for activists gladly accept notices for classes, and often yield promising students. They may even provide materials to support them. Radio stations are effective in reaching a large segment of the public, and most classes can be mentioned in public-service announcements, which are free. Registering with a free, or open, university is also a great way to make contact with those who are looking for classes to take.

Tape-recording class sessions increases the number of people a teacher can reach. One woman in Tucson, Arizona, gives Saturday evening lectures on spiritual awareness and has used this technique effectively. She's arranged for her talks to be aired on the community radio station on Sunday mornings, and as a result, she's expanded her audience tremendously.

Satellite technology and telecommunications have evolved greatly in the past several years. It's now possible to hook up even home seminars with schools and private groups all over the world, so the global sharing of ideas and encouragement is at last a reality.

In many parishes there's a definite need for advisers for individuals seriously interested in joining the Church. As more people express interest in becoming Catholics, and as there are fewer priests to spend time with them for their instruction, a program has been developed through the evangelization program which pairs the inquiring with practicing Catholics. Although much instruction and the final responsibility for the candidate's readiness rests with the priest in charge, the day-to-day questions and problems can be handled by a lay person whose beliefs are in accordance with the Church's teachings.

This system allows for deeper and more personal grounding in the Catholic faith that helps both parties to grow. The pastor of a parish should be contacted to discover if the program is in use there and what preparation is needed to participate.

OFFICE SKILLS • Many small or temporary organizations need offices and staff but simply can't afford them. This is where a homebound person with some extra room and good business skills can really shine. Secretarial talents actually can be used for large groups as well, and those who have them may find that they're in great demand by a number of people.

Typing and filing are very important.

Letters and bulletins need to be typed up regularly, as do reports, proposals, and news releases. The jobs are as time-consuming as they are necessary.

Resource materials must be easy to obtain when they're needed for putting together publicity, etc., so accurate filing is critical. Often, some quick research using up-to-date files may be needed for short-notice press conferences or interviews by members of a group.

Environmental Action coordinator Marni Aaron has suggested, "One way homebound individuals can help is by clipping newspaper articles from their local papers about topics they think might interest us." The idea, of course, applies to any organization or individual who may need ongoing information in a particular field.

Maintaining a specialized library for peace and justice topics is important and can become a ministry in itself. Once material in a certain field begins to accumulate, it can be sorted and assembled for handy reference. Then its availability can be advertised to those who might need it. Some telephone inquiries might even be handled, as well. The possibilities certainly are exciting.

One of the times when office skills are most needed is during elections. Grass-roots politics requires a lot of cooperation and much paperwork. The homebound secretary's skills are more than welcome by candidates who are working on shoestring budgets.

Everyone needs the services of a public notary at one time or another. Becoming one is a significant way to serve both groups and individuals. By making their services available for a minimal fee, or for free, notaries can assist those who need them in a concrete way.

Becoming a notary usually requires little more than obtaining character references, posting a bond, and taking an oath of office, though such requirements may differ from state to state.

GARDENING • Home gardeners can save the world! They can alleviate hunger. They can balance the ecology. They can even break the stranglehold of unjust multinational food producers!

At one time or another, every gardener finds that he has surplus produce. Sharing that extra food with local food banks or with those who are on tight budgets can be a satisfying way to relieve local hunger in a very immediate way.

The fire department in one city in Washington State has mined the resources of home gardeners for several years. The fire fighters have established pickup points where growers can drop off their excess, and then they distribute it to those in need, in cooperation with regional food banks. As a result, tons of high-quality fresh produce get to those who really need it each summer.

Although it's not necessary to have such an elaborate setup in every area, this concrete way of getting food to the hungry is very workable.

There are several ways the home gardener can benefit the ecology, too.

According to the National Wildlife Federation, creative management of even small plots of land has benefited the ecology immensely. Their Backyard Habitat program has been decidedly successful, as those at home have worked to create pockets of healthy environments for dwindling wildlife.

Some members have set up small townhouse plots to encourage butterfly resurgence. Others have planted shrubs and small trees to entice a greater variety of birds, and still others have left sections of their yards wild with natural growth as covers for small animals.

Just planting one tree in a yard improves the environment. Trees modify their immediate areas' heat and cold, absorb noise, significantly reduce air pollution, and provide homes for birds and other wildlife. Nurturing even one small tree can be equivalent to running a neighborhood nature preserve and air-scrubbing operation in one!

Another way for a home gardener to serve the ecology both in the present and in the future is to raise rare, endangered, or ancient species of plants, saving their seeds whenever possible.

Through agribusiness programs, the types of plants grown in this country have dwindled drastically over the last twenty years, as only the most commercially viable varieties are sought. Other less successful breeds are eliminated. Older and wild strains, which are necessary to keep the gene pool large and vigorous, are often lost in the scramble for new hybrids, and only small-scale growers can keep them going. Several seed exchanges for these varieties have sprung up to circulate them, and all are feasible for backyard agriculturalists.

Breaking the back of insensitive multinational food brokers may seem a tall order at first for a homebound gardener. But it's not really as hard as it appears.

Growing our own food as far as possible (even though it may only mean providing herbs from windowsills and tomatoes from large pots) makes us less dependent on the commercial system for our needs. And showing others how to do the same makes *them* equally independent. Sharing the surplus with those who can't grow, and disseminating seeds to others who can, further decreases food-distribution companies' power over neighborhoods. These may seem small actions, but they are essential links in bringing the world down to human scale again.

Even symbolically, gardening can be a force for peace!

In Santa Barbara, California, a Soviet visitor and a U.S. Fellowship of Reconciliation member joined together to plant a peace garden of marigolds for the town.

Those who have the room might want to consider lending small plots in their garden for others to raise their own food. They could set up a community gardening program, and keep tools and seeds available for those who want them. In addition to encouraging some self-sufficiency, then, they could create a pleasant cooperative atmosphere of people raising food together.

So gardening has more impact than it would seem at first, and those at home can be in the vanguard of socially responsible growing.

* * *

From painting to potting, any talents are fair game for the homebound to minister to the needs of the world.

RESOURCES

Boise Peace Quilt Project, P.O. Box 6469, Boise, ID 83707

Cornucopia Project, Rodale Press, 35 E. Minor St., Emmaus, PA 18049 (For help in starting regenerative gardening and agriculture.)

Environmental Action, 1525 New Hampshire Ave., N.W., Washington, DC 20036

- *Sharing Life*
  Heifer Project International, P.O. Box 808, Little Rock, AR 72203 (Has a livestock and small-stock sharing project with the poor of Third World nations.)

The Film Fund, Inc., 80 E. 11th St., New York, NY 10003 (Lobbies for funds, educates and trains independent filmmakers for social change.)

National Gardening Association, 180 Flynn Ave., Burlington, VT 05401

National Wildlife Federation, 1412 16th St., N.W., Washington, DC 20036

Our Lady's Rosary Makers, P.O. Box 37080, Louisville, KY 40233

PeaceNet Computer Link, 1918 Bonita, Berkeley, CA 94704

9
using money

*I want a change
and a radical change.
I want a change
from an acquisitive society
to a functional society,
from a society of go-getters
to a society of go-givers.*

Peter Maurin wrote this "Easy Essay" in the 1930s for Catholic Workers and those interested in the movement. The "Easy Essay" distilled the essence of his attitude toward material possessions, which was directly based on the Gospels.

Today, we, too, must examine seriously our attitude toward money and the way we handle the resources that are given to us. We must pray to be guided in the way we use them, and we must make some difficult, far-reaching decisions.

What we do with money and other goods — whether we give them away, spend them, or even withhold them — can be a vital part of our work for peace and justice.

* * *

Giving money away is the most obvious way to use it for the good of all. The sharing of our cash with those less fortunate than ourselves is important both for them and for us.

The Quaker writer Richard J. Foster, when speaking of giving money away, wrote, "Money . . . is so intimately related to the possessor that one cannot consistently give money without giving self."

We grow spiritually through our donations. And for those who are committed to working for the advance of peace and justice, the act of giving is an essential part of local and global progress.

There are times, though, when contributions seem impossible for the homebound who are on small fixed incomes. Stretching a check to cover thirty days' worth of expenses every month may take all of our ingenuity. But even small amounts are helpful in most cases, and they benefit the giver as much as the receiver.

Gordon Cosby, a minister who's associated with the

Sojourners Community in Washington, D.C., recognizes that fact. And he tells the following story to support his statement that the poor suffer as much from the fact that they're not able to give as they do from having a lack of funds.

Once, when Cosby was the pastor of a small congregation in a mountain town of Virginia, his deacon approached him about a "problem" they had with a member of the congregation. She was a widow with six children, yet she insisted on tithing her small income to the church. She obviously couldn't afford it, and the deacon, along with other members, urged him as pastor to go and advise her that she was relieved of her financial obligation to the church.

Cosby did, and when he'd finished she answered him heartbrokenly, "I want to tell you that you are taking away the last thing that gives my life dignity and meaning."

In the New Testament, Christ watched another widow drop her last mites (the equivalent of a few pennies) into the collection box and didn't try to stop her, or even reimburse her for it. Instead, He praised her for giving out of her necessity, rather than her surplus. He taught His Apostles the lesson of real giving through her example.

Generosity isn't just recommended, though — it's mandated by the rules of love in both the Old and New Testaments.

St. John Chrysostom wrote these stern words to the members of the early Church, "You eat to excess; Christ eats not even what He needs. . . . You drink fine wine;

but on Him you have not bestowed so much as a cup of cold water. You lie on a soft and embroidered bed; but He is perishing in the cold. . . . Don't you realize you are going to be held accountable?"

But where and how must our money go to be most effective? Our mailboxes quickly fill with solicitations for every cause from "Feeding the Starving Africans" to "Saving the Whales." Each cause is worthy, and all of them tug at the heart of any concerned person.

Our first move should be to remember our commitments. In the beginning, we decided that although there were hundreds of issues needing our time and effort, we, to be most effective, had to concentrate on one or two areas only. The same holds true in sharing material resources.

We can pick our charities, rather than waiting for them to present themselves to us through the mail. Writing to organizations or individuals that are carrying out what we feel to be worthy works will usually bring a prompt response along with suggestions as to how they can best be assisted. Libraries can supply the addresses of most of these groups.

Unsolicited requests that arrive through the mail can be sorted and dumped if they're not in our area of action. This may make us feel guilty for a while, but it's absolutely necessary to help us keep our focus on our true commitments.

Ongoing contributions are often more effective than scattershot donations of a few dollars here and there. A pledged monthly amount, even though small, will often help a group to accurately project its budget. By giving small amounts on a regular basis, donors can usually end up supplying more than they'd originally planned, which is a boon to those who are receiving it.

Our parish churches shouldn't be forgotten here. They can only serve the people if they are solvent and have enough funds to run needed programs. Moreover, those funds must be supplied by the parishioners insofar as they are able.

Adoption programs are popular with many groups. Children, grandmothers, nuns, priests, and even whales are up for sponsorship these days! Monthly contributions help to keep them going, and in some cases, even assist the adoptees' entire communities. One of the values of these programs is that (except, obviously, in the case of animals) sponsors can correspond with their adopted persons, resulting in long-term, deep relationships that go far beyond the benefit of money alone.

Through Methodists for Life, Dr. Olga Fairfax has suggested sponsoring a needy pregnant mother for her term and immediately afterward in order to make her commitment easier for her.

Members of Sojourners call for their peacemaking groups to financially support those who give up careers in the weapons industry to pursue more peaceful occupations until they're able to make a go of it on their own.

But there are other things to sponsor as well, and they can lead to some exciting results.

Writing contests, poster competitions, scholastic prizes, and such can be a great way to stimulate thinking on an issue in a community and to "spread the word" about a particular problem. Prizes need not be large to encourage participation either, especially among the young, who often benefit the most from such incentives.

Anyone can run contests like these. They can be promoted through an existing group, or by only one person. Though they require some thought as to rules, limitations, judges (if there are to be any other than the sponsor), and so on, they can be a definite force for good in an area.

For those who have the funds also, offering scholarships for needy students to continue their education in fields that will benefit the human race may do a great amount of good. Even a one-year scholarship of one hundred dollars may be enough to enable a promising student to start college.

Protesters often run afoul of the law in doing what they feel is right, and refugees who come to this country unprepared often need cash for their legal expenses. A concerned citizen can pay these costs for them, helping justice be done in this way. One example of someone who did this was Virginia Foster Dunn. The recipient of the Common Cause Public Service Achievement Award in 1985, she and her husband provided the bail for Rosa Parks in 1959 when the latter was arrested for refusing to give her seat to a white man on a Birmingham bus. The result of that action, of course, was the beginning of the civil-rights movement.

Gift-giving times, such as Christmas and birthdays, are great opportunities to make donations to various causes. Giving money to honor a friend or relative is a responsible and fun way to bestow a meaningful present — and to benefit programs that will help the world we live in. To encourage the practice, many organizations (including Catholic Relief Services) have attractive cards to announce the gift.

Other meaningful gifts are gift certificates from organizations and copies of their catalogs. Many groups have T-shirts, books, posters and other artwork, etc., and offer them by mail. UNICEF has both shops and mail-order services, for example, and Greenpeace offers a complete line of clothing to finance its work.

Gift memberships in groups are also often welcome. Paying others' dues for the first year of their affiliation can start them on the path of being active and finding their own way of involvement.

But giving needn't stop even at death!

Bequests are another way to spread our wealth. They're made as part of a will and can be done in a variety of ways.

Outright gifts or restricted donations that rely on certain stipulations are two of the most used. But there are many ways to include an organization in a will, so it's best to consult a lawyer as to the form that's closest to what you have in mind. If a will has already been drawn, it can be modified by adding a codicil.

A number of groups have planned giving options, which provide tax-free income during the lifetime of the giver, as well as benefiting the groups at the time of that person's death.

* * *

Cash isn't the only thing we can give to charity, though. There are several groups that can use things we might otherwise discard, or who can profit from our surplus.

The residents of St. Francis Retirement Village in Crowley, Texas, meet regularly to sort and organize the canceled commemorative stamps that donors send to them. These stamps are then sold to dealers for resale, and the community uses the money to benefit all who live there.

Missions can also use canceled stamps to add ever needed funds to their coffers.

Some soup-can labels and trading stamps are valuable to schools and other facilities that redeem them for much needed items such as athletic equipment and sickroom materials. Local schools have drives periodically for these articles, and some missions in the United States ask for donations through national appeals.

Books are sought-after items. Libraries often solicit used books for their collections as well as for sales that raise much needed money to continue their services.

Connecticut's Darien Book Aid Plan provides books to those living overseas as well as to those in the U.S. who need them. Foreign libraries, universities, teachers, etc., receive them free of charge, as do day care and correctional centers in this country. They have firm requirements as to what volumes they will take, but those they do accept are well used.

Most libraries, whether public or private, welcome magazine subscriptions. Gifts of periodicals that promote peace or justice are excellent donations and serve two purposes at once. They educate the public and help small libraries, especially, to build up their collections.

Resource centers in schools, prisons, and churches are among those that are most appreciative of this type of offering.

Missions can use materials, but it's best not to send goods to them directly because of the heavy duties many countries impose on articles shipped in from the outside. Contacting the U.S. branch of the missions is the best way to find out what they need and how to get the goods to those who require them.

The needy are close to home, too. Food banks, social service agencies, and fire departments often need extra food, clothing, blankets, and toys, especially during local crises or after disasters. Even such occurrences as strikes can make a heavy demand on those who provide for the poor.

The St. Vincent de Paul Society and the Salvation Army routinely solicit donations for their works, too, and will arrange to pick them up at a donor's home.

Buying an extra can of food for the needy on shopping day is one way to make a painless and meaningful donation. And adding it to similar gifts from others can make a real difference in the quality of life for the hungry of cities and poorer rural areas alike.

One Chicago woman organized a monthly food collection in her neighborhood just by sending notes to her neighbors asking them if they could spare an item or two a month for the hungry. The response was overwhelming. She collected donations regularly herself, though some people left their goods off at her home. She then bagged the contributions and took them to a nearby settlement house.

The ongoing program has been so successful that the workers there told her, "If every neighborhood did this, there would be no hungry people left to feed!"

Her project is very adaptable for those who are homebound, too. They can serve as organizers and collection points for food donations. Once the collections are bagged, volunteers can be recruited to take the packages to food banks, Catholic Worker houses, or soup kitchens where they're warmly received.

Finally, there's the ultimate sacrifice. Although the idea may seem macabre to many, donating our bodies and organs for research or reuse after death is an outstanding way to show concern for the ongoing world.

There's a tremendous need for corneas, organs, bones, and tissues for transplants every year.

According to the transplant coordinator of the University Medical Center in Tucson, Arizona, there's a critical need for people who are willing to give their organs. Each transplant team has a waiting list of recipients whose needs are immediate. In 1985 alone, for example, nine hundred sixty-two heart transplants were done in centers around the world and many more were needed.

Even if one or more parts in a donor's body are damaged, such as the heart or lungs, other parts may be used, such as the corneas or bone marrow.

Medical schools can use the bodies of both previously healthy and diseased people. Students learn much from examining both and they are the doctors of the future. So donating one's body for research can eventually help others to live healthier, longer lives.

* * *

But giving away money and possessions isn't the only way to use our resources for the good of mankind. Spending money responsibly — and even choosing not to spend it in certain circumstances — can be a powerful way to serve the world.

We Americans are great consumers. Study after study shows that we use a disproportionate amount of the world's resources — at great expense to both the environment and many poor countries that provide for our "needs." Many of our "fast food" burgers, for example, are made from beef that's raised on pasture created by the destruction of tropical rain forests. And the people of at least one Central American nation aren't able to raise food for themselves on small farms because their land has been taken over by big coffee companies that supply the American coffeepot.

What should our first actions be, then?

We can begin by reducing our demand for unnecessary or luxury items that are hurting the land and people who produce them. We can learn to live more simply.

Living simply isn't as easy as it sounds.

First, it involves an honest evaluation of the way we're living currently. Next, it calls for making changes based on our findings. Both of these are difficult.

There are no hard-and-fast rules to evaluating our lives. What for some might be a luxury (for example, a VCR and a TV set) may be for others a necessity. Those who are homebound and have few other sources of entertainment, or those with children who can benefit from monitored entertainment, may find a VCR and a TV set very useful. And to those who've chosen to make tapes for the local public-access channel, of course, they are essential. We must try to honestly judge each of our purchases on the basis of real need.

All of us need to reevaluate our eating habits. Exotic sweets and gourmet brands of vegetables can often be replaced with homemade or fresh alternatives that are just as good and less expensive.

Meat isn't necessary three times a day and can even be harmful in large quantities. It's been estimated that if Americans reduced their meat consumption by just ten percent, we could feed the entire population of India with the surplus grain. So we need to examine the ultimate costs of the purchase we make in the food stores.

For the past thirteen years an organization called Alternatives, headquartered in Ellenwood, Georgia, has been promoting "voluntary simplicity" for those interested. The organization urges that all consumers base their buying habits on the criteria of necessity, ecology, self-sufficiency, and social responsibility.

That means that pertinent questions to ask before buying a product should be:

✓ Do I really need this?

✓ Does it hurt the land to produce this?

✓ Are there any alternatives I can buy or make that won't be so harmful?

✓ Does this product make me more dependent on big business or the system (such as buying something that requires a great deal of electricity, which will entail relying more on a public utility)?

✓ Does this item come from a company that treats its workers fairly?

If the answers are satisfactory on all counts, it's fairly safe to go ahead and buy it. If not, it's time to examine viable alternatives.

Doing without, whether it be a meal, a luxury item, or even a necessity, and donating the money to someone who is in need is a responsible and praiseworthy action.

"Use it up. Wear it out. Make it do, or do without."

It's an old adage and was especially common during World War II when rationing was necessary. Today, for the sake of peace, it's just as pertinent.

An integral part of living simply is recycling. This popular practice of the seventies has gone pretty much by the board these days; but it's still valid — and always necessary for environmental reasons.

Nearly every article that comes into a home can be used more than once. But if not, it can be sent to a recycling center where it can be reprocessed. Plastic bags, cardboard boxes, and grocery sacks can be reused right in the home, while metal cans, newspapers, and glass containers can be sent to recycling centers in most towns.

Scout troops and similar young people's organizations will often pick up recyclables so that they can earn money for their activities by selling them. Even organic wastes, such as vegetable peelings and leftovers, can be composted by those with gardens, to turn into soil to raise more food.

Saving energy is as important in the 1980s as it was during the "energy crisis" of 1974. Utility companies must still pollute the environment to provide electricity for their customers, so it stands to reason that the less demand they have to meet, the less they'll need to pollute to deliver it.

Specters of the Soviet Union's disaster at Chernobyl dog every request for new nuclear power plants these days. More and more consumers are asking if such dangerous ways of supplying their needs are really called for. One very effective method to discourage the construction of nuclear power facilities in the future is to decrease demand for the power companies' services.

According to the Nuclear Information and Resource Center, a simple program of weatherization for homes (including caulking, weatherstripping, and furnace tune-ups) would save this country "almost *twice* the net output of all the nuclear reactors operating in the country today!"

"While Congress debates energy policy, while courts and learned experts discuss environmental trade-offs, while economists pontificate, people in their own communities can do something to help themselves," wrote the late David Lilienthal, former chairman of the Tennessee Valley Authority and the Atomic Energy Commission.

He was speaking about the fact that individuals can really be the solution for what may seem to be giant problems in this area. Turning off a bathroom light when it's not in use may seem insignificant, but when it's multiplied by hundreds or thousands of others doing the same, it can be a determining factor in whether a new power plant should be built in a community.

Bruce Stokes, the author of *Helping Ourselves*, adds, "The energy future can be determined democratically through energy conservation" — and that means through the actions of each citizen.

* * *

Not spending money is an interesting way to affect the world, too. Buying less to satisfy our needs, boycotting, and tax resistance all are techniques in non-spending that are especially effective.

Perhaps the two best known boycotts in recent history are the California grape boycott of the seventies and the Nestlé's boycott in the early eighties. Both were very successful and made immense gains for both exploited migrant farm workers and for the exploited mothers of the Third World. But others, less well publicized, have had just as dramatic results.

Campbell's Soup Company was boycotted for months because of poor working conditions in the fields of its Ohio suppliers. Campbell's finally did respond, and as a result the workers' lives are now considerably improved. Coca-Cola divested itself of its holdings in South Africa only weeks after a boycott was called to encourage that action.

In its 1976 General Assembly, the American Medical Association passed a resolution suggesting that its members urge patients to boycott the sponsors of violent TV shows, as the programs were shown to be severe health hazards.

The most effective way to participate in a boycott is to write a letter first to the company or companies that are going to be affected. They must know that they are being boycotted, and why. Simply not buying their brand won't affect their sales tremendously, unless they're local merchants, but if they connect fewer sales with the letters they receive, they'll be quicker to correct an unjust situation.

In a churchyard on a busy street corner in Tucson stands a huge red-and-black sign with the startling message, "It's a Sin to Pay for a Nuclear Weapon."

The thought is clear enough, and it has made many people reflect on their involvement with the nuclear weapons buildup through the simple act of paying their taxes.

Tax resistance is very serious business, and it must be undertaken with a lot of forethought and prayer. The consequences can be stiff, even though the reasons for participating in it may be sincere and profound. But many people who object to war as a method of international problem solving, or simply to the stockpiling of nuclear weapons, should seriously consider removing their dollars from a system that supports it.

Several groups are available to help those who feel they can no longer support the government financially.

But there is at least one reasonably "safe" way of depriving the weapons builders of their money. It's called "phone tax withholding."

The Federal excise tax on telephone calls was established in World War II and has been kept specifically to finance the U.S. Department of Defense through the years. It has been raised and lowered as the country has been in and out of wars but has never been repealed. It's possible to refuse to pay the tax, and run virtually no chance of being prosecuted as long as certain procedures are followed, since the amount for each person is normally so small.

The money saved can be given to any number of peace or welfare organizations at the end of the year, so real benefit follows from this type of protest. War Tax Resistance groups can give interested people more information.

* * *

Money, as you can see, is a formidable tool in creating a just and peaceful world. Spending it, giving it away, or withholding it from those we feel are abusing their financial power are all valid ways of making money "talk" for the right reasons.

RESOURCES

Alternatives, Box 429, 5233 Bouldercrest Rd., Ellenwood, GA 30049

Citizens' Energy Project, 1110 6th St., N.W., Washington, DC 20001

Citizens for Tax Justice, 2020 K St., N.W., Washington, DC 20066

Conscience and Military Tax Campaign, 44 Bellhaven Rd., Bellport, NY 11713

Co-op America, 2100 M St., N.W., Suite 605, Washington, DC 20063 (Catalog sales for goods and services produced by socially and ecologically responsible companies.)

Darien Book Aid Plan, 1926 Post Rd., Darien, CT 06820

Donor Clearing House, The Living Bank, P.O. Box 6725, Houston, TX 77022

Food for the Hungry, 7729 E. Greenway Rd., Scottsdale, AZ 85260 (Has a child sponsorship program called Everychild.)

Franciscan Missions, Inc., P.O. Box 130, Waterford, WI 53185 (Accepts sewing supplies, canceled stamps, coins, and jewelry.)

National Campaign for a Peace Tax Fund, 2121 Decatur Pl., N.W., Washington, DC 20008

National Recycling Coalition, Inc., 45 Rockefeller Plaza, Rm. 2530, New York, NY 10111

Oxfam-America, 115 Broadway, Boston, MA 02116

Prison Book Program, 92 Green St., Jamaica Plain, MA 02130

St. Francis Retirement Village, Chapel Plaza, Crowley, TX 76036 (Accepts canceled stamps.)

Save the Children, 54 Wilton Rd., Westport, CT 06880

University of Arizona, 1501 N. Campbell Ave., Rm. 4402, Tucson, AZ 85724 (Has information on becoming an organ and tissue donor.)

War Tax Resistance Coordinating Committee, P.O. Box 2236, East Patchogue, NY 11772 (Has information on phone tax resistance as well as other tax resistance.)

JustLife, P.O. Box 15263, Washington, DC 20003

League of Conservation Voters, 320 Fourth St., N.E., Washington, DC 20002 (Political arm of the environmental movement.)

10
miscellaneous

CITIZENSHIP • It's easy to lose sight of the fact that in the United States, the people *are* the government!

Although it's not possible for everyone to go to Washington and actually vote on individual bills or participate in congressional debates, most of the actions necessary to keep a democracy functioning still belong to the public.

Voting in elections is immensely important — but only thirty-eight percent of all eligible voters in this country cast their ballots each election day!

The ballot is the basic tool of keeping this country free, and using it responsibly is the main way citizens have of keeping officials responsive and accountable. But since only a third of the people use their votes, most officials are elected and most laws are made by a small minority.

Like it or not, voting is an obligation of citizenship — not just a privilege.

For those who can't get out of their homes, absentee ballots are readily available. Contacting representatives of any political party is the best way to get one. In many areas, they'll even arrange transportation to the polls for those who can't otherwise make it there.

Primaries and local elections are just as important as national contests. Because regional laws and statutes affect our everyday lives more than most national legislation does, we must make a real effort to participate in regional campaigns, bond issues, etc.

Federal and state governments provide broad guidelines governing schools, for example, but the decisions controlling what's actually taught, who the teachers are, and what texts are used, belong to city or town school boards. And what the children in an area are taught determines to a great extent how they think about the world.

So school board elections, which are often thought of as throwaway offices, are critical to our future as a nation.

Father James Keller, founder of the Christophers, wrote, "Whether it is a national, primary or school board election, your vote means more than you realize. Never forget — the absent are always wrong."

Any U.S. citizen can have a bill introduced to Congress!

If an individual or a group of people, after study and serious thought, find that they feel the country would benefit from a law, they can present their requirements to their congressional representative.

The proposal may be written in plain language, because it will be submitted immediately to the Office of Legislative Counsel, which will draft it in proper legalese. It's then a part of a congressman's job to introduce his constituent's bills to the proper committee.

Although getting a citizen's bill acted on requires a lot of hard work (including frequent follow-ups with the sponsor, getting good publicity, and rounding up strong support), the rewards in having it passed are worth it — and it may make the nation more responsive to real needs.

According to the office of Rep. Morris Udall, a Democrat from Arizona, it's also possible for a private citizen to get something read into the *Congressional Record*.

The citizen should write to one or more sympathetic representatives asking that the enclosed information be read into the *Record*. Although they may not have the time or opportunity to do so, most congressmen will try to comply, and when they do, the information will become part of the permanent written record of the U.S. Congress!

Elected officials have a duty to work for their constituents. Though they can't work miracles, they *can* cut red tape, prod sluggish bureaucracies, and be advocates for helpless constituents.

Ordinary people can often accomplish the same thing, though, if they know how to "work the system."

For those who are interested and challenged by the thought of helping others, becoming an unofficial "ombudsman" for a neighborhood may be a rewarding option.

The job requires nothing more than becoming familiar with how government works, whom to talk to in certain circumstances, and how to contact the proper authorities when needed. It calls for a great deal of self-organization as well as plenty of tenacity and a high frustration threshold!

There's tremendous satisfaction in working for others this way, and seeing knotty problems solved in just and equitable ways. Ombudsmen bring the nation closer to the Founding Fathers' ideal of "justice for all."

ON THE LIGHT SIDE • Working for peace and justice isn't all serious, solemn, and tough, though. Sometimes it's fun and doesn't require much labor at all.

Election times mean partisan support, and one way to back a stand is to put signs on the lawn and placards in the window. Signs can boost candidates or push propositions, but either way they get their messages across with little or no work involved. Whether they're homemade or professionally done makes no difference in their effectiveness either.

Making them may be a good way to practice the graphics skills mentioned in an earlier chapter.

Part of the fun involved in campaigning is to pass out buttons and bumper stickers to those who appear at our doors, be they neighbor, salesman, or survey-taker. Even Halloween trick-or-treaters are good targets for colorful "propaganda" materials!

The night before an election is a critical one for all hopefuls. At this time, those at home can make calls to remind others to vote and, incidentally, mention the name of their candidate. Most campaign offices will send possible "scripts" to be used as well as a list of numbers that need to be contacted.

Many groups such as Greenpeace and Witness for Peace send copies of petitions from time to time for their members to fill with signatures. They may be supporting an Antarctic world park, or asking Congress to vote justly on Central American issues, but they need to be completed to be effective.

A fine way to accomplish this is to keep petitions near the door and ask those who show up to sign them. Though some will be hesitant, many will be delighted to have such a simple and painless way to speak out for their beliefs.

Library books carry a great deal of food for thought. Each one reaches many readers and has real impact on their thoughts. And we can add to their usefulness. Just before returning our selections, we can stuff "message" bookmarks among their pages. Though some may be detected and removed by alert librarians, many of them will get through the check-in process. They'll be seen and read by many patrons — both those who check books out, and those who are just browsing. Bookmarks, like placards, can be homemade or purchased from concerned groups.

Brochures and pamphlets are inexpensive forums for many groups and individuals. They carry arguments and inspiration in a quick, easy-to-read format, and they're usually quite cheap in small quantities. Moreover, they can be ordered by mail to be distributed at one's leisure. The homebound can send them out individually or in packets to friends. They can arrange to have others drop off quantities in various public areas where those interested can pick them up. Or they can send some to the media requesting that they investigate and report on the information given.

However they're used, these printed materials are excellent means of spreading the truth.

HODGEPODGE • Rep. Robert Kastenmeier, a Wisconsin Democrat, has declared himself a nuclear-free zone. He's registered with Nukewatch and has notified government agencies of his decision. Many others have joined him.

Individuals, homes, farms, schools, neighborhoods, cities (such as Sykesville, Maryland, and Ashland, Oregon), states, and countries (New Zealand and Wales, for example) have all declared themselves nuclear-free zones just by announcing the fact. They have stated, in a number of ways, that they do not welcome any nuclear weapons or activities which lead to the same within their boundaries. They renounce all rights to be "defended" by nukes (as nuclear weapons, etc., are called) and insist that they be taken off any target lists because of this.

These declarations are symbolic and can't really be enforced, except by nations like New Zealand, which declared nuclear-free status in 1986. But they are constructive in bringing the weapons issues to light and in influencing politicians in their decisions.

All nuclear-free zones can be registered with Nukewatch, which keeps a tally of those in the U.S. It also provides appropriate stickers and decals to identify declared areas. Notification should also be sent to governmental representatives in order to be most effective.

Animal-rights groups often rescue animals from laboratories and research institutes. They're always on the lookout for homes for these creatures and welcome all offers. Animal lovers might consider volunteering with local groups, or write to the central office of PETA (People for the Ethical Treatment of Animals) to offer their services.

Private shelters for the homeless often need homemaking services such as laundry, mending, and the like. Arrangements can be made by contacting them. Baking cookies and special treats for soup kitchens and shelters and having the goodies picked up can also brighten the days of the less fortunate.

The sightless aren't illiterate, but they do need special books to keep up with events. Through the services of the Library of Congress, home volunteers who can use braille typewriters are given "translating" work to do. The skill is relatively easy to learn and can add quality to the lives of the visually impaired.

* * *

With some creativity, and a real desire to serve the world, anyone can add to this list of suggestions. Many times, through working for others, individuals will discover new talents and energies in themselves that they hadn't suspected before.

RESOURCES

Archbishop Fulton J. Sheen Angel Award Committee, Catholic Media Center, P.O. Box 18081, Tampa, FL 33679 (Accepts applications for award made to those working in newspaper, radio, television, or advertising who have made a "unique contribution to the understanding of the God-given worth of the human being.")

Campaign for a People's Peace Treaty, 1140 Broadway, Rm. 401, New York, NY 10001 (Has petitions for a people's peace treaty available.)

League of Women Voters of the U.S., 1346 Connecticut Ave., N.W., Washington, DC 20036

Martin Luther King, Jr., Award Committee, Fellowship of Reconciliation, Box 271, Nyack, NY 10960 (Accepts applications for award made to a person or group making a significant contribution to the nonviolent struggle for a peaceful and just society.)

National Library Service for the Blind and Physically Handicapped, Library of Congress, Washington, DC 20542

Nukewatch, 315 W. Gorham St., Madison, WI 53703 (Has applications for and registers nuclear-free zones.)

People for the Ethical Treatment of Animals, P.O. Box 42516, Washington, DC 20015

Witness for Peace, P.O. Box 29497, Washington, DC 20017

11
joining groups

Recently, the Fellowship of Reconciliation (FOR) awarded special certificates to those who had been members for over fifty years. On this momentous occasion, these stalwarts shared their thoughts about having been part of the group for that long.

"The FOR is . . . apt to spot a need earlier than most others and to get busy with a creative plan for dealing with the situation," one pointed out.

Another said, "To us, FOR has . . . been our . . . continuing beacon of guidance through many a tangled social issue."

A third added that "the FOR is a support group that helps us keep our faith."

Working for social justice or any of the peace or environmental issues is tough work. Frustrations abound. It's difficult to keep abreast of every development that needs attention. And some issues become so complex that we end up unsure if we're supporting the right stand at all! Many workers wind up feeling lonely and isolated from the people around them.

Trying to deal alone with all of these factors is often hard, if not impossible. Even those who feel they're "loners" must at some point recognize their need for others. That's why working together is one way to make sure the job gets done.

The authors of *Who Runs Congress? A Citizen's Handbook to Government* recognize that fact and encourage their readers to associate themselves with existing organizations.

"A group is more likely to have the resources and endurance to carry a seemingly interminable project through to completion," they write. "A group can commit more energy and resources than even the most dedicated individual."

The initial reason that usually prompts a person to join an organization is to learn more about the cause he or she supports. Through their newsletters, notes, position papers, etc., an association can keep a member well-grounded and up-to-date in its field. The fact that there are several members means also that they can gather and share more information more easily than can one person exploring the issue alone.

Because of the diversity of people in a group, too, it's possible to brainstorm various problems and come up with solutions and actions that might never have occurred to an individual. Creativity in dealing with situations seems to increase in direct proportion to the number of people involved in examining them. So our effectiveness is expanded as we join with others.

Brainstorming also assists in "clarifying thought," as the Catholic Worker Movement's Peter Maurin would have said. Intense discussion of issues helps to bring half-formed questions and opinions out into the open for full examination. Turning questions around and probing them from many viewpoints to see new facets of their entirety also aids in our understanding and discernment.

Organizations can eliminate early burnout by encouraging the division of labor.

Whether it's a small local group or a large national organization, any association of people can split up into task groups to ease the load of individual members. Because each one can then do the work that most appeals to the individual, nearly every effort becomes rewarding, and valuable energies aren't bogged down in grinding or inappropriate chores. Ideally, these groups will then work together to complement each other.

In really cooperative groups, too, members can teach one another their skills and reinforce the work of one another regularly. Leaders of such organizations have found that the output of the various members often totals more than the sum of their individual efforts.

Another major reason for joining existing groups is the benefit that comes from mutual support.

The frequent defeats and setbacks in working for any reform can cause a single worker to lose heart. But if such workers can share their discouragement, or hear from others who've overcome similar blows, they can often find the strength to continue.

The War Resisters League writes, "As a member of a group, you can absorb failures more easily and failures can lead to future successes when the group evaluates what happened and why."

Just "unloading" to someone who understands the situation is therapeutic. And the results often lead to healing laughter. Sharing with others helps us to put our experiences in context.

One needn't be physically present at meetings to be a member of an organization, though.

Many groups, especially on the national and international level, function well by having a cadre of field workers supported by and in touch with those at home. Regular publications keep all members in contact with one another. Their articles and letters encourage members to "keep on keeping on," as well as to share vital information with one another.

* * *

Today, there are groups that address nearly every legitimate concern — or so it seems. Amnesty International works for human rights. Bread for the World acts on hunger questions. The Nature Conservancy fights for environmental protection. The National Peace Institute Foundation supports creative conflict resolution. The National Coalition on Television Violence watchdogs the media. The list is endless.

But there are times when new needs surface that must be addressed collectively. Limited local issues, too — although restricted in their appeal — can benefit from citizens working together to solve them.

When Gandhi was confronted with South Africa's restrictive laws against minorities during his first visit there as a young lawyer, he was stunned to realize that there were no organizations in place to fight them. It was then that he began his programs of cooperation among the repressed. "I am a man possessed by an idea," he said. "If such a man cannot get an organization, he becomes an organization."

In forming an effective group, it's essential for the organizers to have clear objectives and a well thought-out plan of action, with room enough for input from all members and a reasonable amount of work for each one to do. Though money is very helpful, it isn't the overriding concern that many professional authorities would have us believe. Dedication and hard work are far more effective in the long run.

Ad hoc committees and coalitions for short-term projects are formed regularly and accomplish a lot. It doesn't matter whether they begin in someone's kitchen or in the board room of a social-action agency. As a matter of fact, the most effective committees and organizations often begin over a cup of coffee.

The Catholic Workers began over a kitchen table in the New York City apartment of Dorothy Day's sister. It was there that Dorothy Day and Peter Maurin had their first discussions of theory, which evolved into the birth of the Catholic Worker publication in May, 1933.

And Jean Vanier, the founder of L'Arche (an international movement dealing with the needs of the physically and mentally disabled), was sparked by a fireside conversation he had with his confessor. At the priest's urging, he arranged to have two retarded men share his house. They formed the core for the first L'Arche community, and the idea spread quickly from there.

* * *

Some people who've been working alone and diligently for their cause experience a letdown when they join groups with the same aims. They become disenchanted with the leadership, frustrated with the seemingly petty details and conflicts that go on, and disconcerted by the amount of time and effort spent on keeping the organization going, rather than achieving goals. Even the group's methods of attacking problems may baffle them.

The most realistic way to deal with these problems is to understand that as long as people are involved, no situation will be ideal. It's true of the Church, schools, and governments, and small idealistic groups are no exception. Daily frictions and misunderstandings are part of life, and they can become magnified in a close group setting. Because no two people view situations from exactly the same vantage point, there's bound to be disagreement on priorities and methods.

When joining a group we must choose to ignore the minor irritations in an effort to achieve the worthwhile goals that drew us toward them. We must learn to forgive perceived slights, keep to our original vision, and continue to work toward stated goals.

We must also examine a group carefully before joining it to see if it's really in tune with our convictions. We should be familiar not only with its goals but also with the methods it espouses to reach its aims.

An environmentalist who believes in working through the system, for example, might consider joining the Sierra Club Legal Defense Fund, which brings violators of national standards to court and uses the legal system of redress. But the same person would hardly be satisfied in supporting the EarthFirst group, which advocates the use of direct action against polluters and developers. The aims of both groups are the same (protecting the environment), but their techniques are vastly different. And both need dedicated members who are aware of and willing to assist their work.

So it's wise to send for information on any group that sounds interesting before joining. Watch the news and scan various magazines for any references to the organization in question. Also talk to some of its members, if there is a local branch. Only then will it become clear if this is a group that will be easy to work with.

Another problem in joining a group is our possible loss of initiative. The more we identify with an organization, the more we tend to follow its programs, rather than striking out on our own.

Waiting for the hierarchy to assign work before acting can reduce us to being dues payers only. We mustn't lose the vision that originally prompted us to join with the group. It's necessary to maintain our momentum, even though an action may not be specifically initiated by a group. It's important to remember that we don't give up our individual rights when joining an organization.

They merely add to the effectiveness of what we're already doing.

The only rule to observe when engaging in individual work is to use the organization's name to endorse our actions *only* with their specific permission. If the organization supports us, so much the better; but identifying ourselves as its members, and then taking part in actions the group objects to, can obstruct the organization in reaching its goals as well as reducing our own effectiveness.

Members of organizations have responsibilities, too. They should support the group not only financially but also with their energies. They need to offer input whenever it would be helpful. They should discuss problems with those involved, rather than airing grievances outside the group first.

All of these considerations help make groups more effective and more able to advance their causes more efficiently.

* * *

So "to join or not to join" is really *not* the question! The real question is how many and which groups to support.

RESOURCES

Action for Children's Television, 2 University Rd., Cambridge, MA 02138

American Coalition of Citizens with Disabilities, 1200 15th St., N.W., Suite 201, Washington, DC 20005

Beyond War, 222 High St., Palo Alto, CA 94301

Bread for the World, 802 Rhode Island Ave., N.E., Washington, DC 20018

Catholic League for Religious and Civil Rights, 1100 W. Wells, Milwaukee, WI 53233

Common Cause, 2030 M St., N.W., Washington, DC 20036

Community for Creative Non-Violence, 1345 Euclid St., N.W., Washington, DC 20009

Fellowship of Reconciliation, Box 271, Nyack, NY 10960

Friends of the Earth, 1045 Sansome St., San Francisco, CA 94105

For Love of Children, 1711 14th St., N.W., Washington, DC 20009 (Works for abused children.)

Gray Panthers, 3700 Chestnut St., Philadelphia, PA 19104 (Works for rights of the aged.)

Greenpeace U.S.A., 1611 Connecticut Ave., N.W., Washington, DC 20009

JustLife, P.O. Box 15263, Washington, DC 20003

League of Conservation Voters, 320 Fourth St., N.E., Washington, DC 20002 (Political arm of the environmental movement.)

Mothers Against Drunk Drivers (MADD), 669 Airport Freeway, Suite 310, Hurst, TX 76053

National Association for the Advancement of Colored People (NAACP), 186 Remsen St., Brooklyn, NY 11201

National Audubon Society, 950 Third Ave., New York, NY 10022

National Citizens Coalition for Nursing Home Reform, 1309 L St., N.W., Washington, DC 20005

National Coalition on Television Violence, P.O. Box 2157, Champaign, IL 61820

National Peace Institute Foundation, 110 Maryland Ave., N.E., Washington, DC 20002

National Right to Life, 419 Seventh St., N.W., Washington, DC 20004

Offender Aid and Restoration of the U.S., 409 E. High St., Charlottesville, VA 22901

Pax Christi U.S.A., 348 E. 10th St., Erie, PA 16503

People for the Ethical Treatment of Animals, P.O. Box 42516, Washington, DC 20015

Public Citizens Health Research Group, 2000 P St., N.W., Washington, DC 20036 (Lobbies for health-care reform.)

Rural America Coalition, 1302 18th St., N.W., No. 302, Washington, DC 20036

Witness for Peace, P.O. Box 29497, Washington, DC 20017

Women's International League for Peace and Freedom, 1213 Race St., Philadelphia, PA 19107

12
burnout

Cops experience it.
So do nurses.
Many teachers are victims of it, too.
Even homemakers suffer from it.

Sooner or later, everyone experiences burnout to some degree, and those who work for peace and justice or other causes aren't immune. They are, actually, prime targets for the malady. As a matter of fact, according to research, the more idealistic such individuals are when they start a project, the more prone they are to burning out after a time.

Working to change the world can be terribly frustrating and depressing. Because success depends on a radical change in most of the population, progress goes very slowly, and the setbacks are frequent. Elections of the "right" candidates slip through our fingers, and anti-pollution victories are diluted by slick legal maneuvers that render them almost trivial.

The result?

Burnout.

Its symptoms are irritability, depression, a feeling of worthlessness, and exhaustion. Life seems to be drained of its purpose, and there's just not much stimulus to continue. Actions that once seemed exciting and important no longer do — as a matter of fact, they appear hopelessly idealistic or meaningless. The world seems pretty bleak in spite of all the hard work by so many dedicated people.

Even those other people appear to be annoyances; their demands are just harassments and the burned-out try to avoid them as well as any other reminder of the issues. The urge to drop it all becomes overwhelming. But even attempting to escape fills them with guilt, and they grow more depressed, more burned out by it.

One characteristic of the volunteers at Catholic Worker Houses, some of the most dedicated advocates for change in the social system, is their susceptibility to burnout.

"They come with stars in their eyes," Dorothy Day once wrote, "and leave with curses on their lips."

But the situation isn't hopeless!

Burnout is *not* a terminal condition.

Burnout, quite simply, is a temporary loss of balance. It comes from focusing on one spot too long without respite. It causes loss of perspective and vertigo of the spirit.

Certain remedies suggest themselves immediately.

The first is prayer.

Father Bruce Ritter of Covenant House, a shelter and advocacy center for runaways in New York City, insists that his staff take time for prayer every day. Without that, he says, their work is ungrounded and ultimately useless. In fact, as he points out, his workers can stand up to the shocks of the job longer when they pray daily.

Jesus said, "Come to me, all who labor and are heavy laden, and I will give you rest" (Matthew 11:28). Through prayer and meditation, we do just that. The resulting refreshment and strength are invaluable.

Daily prayer and meditation time serve to center us on God, without whom no work would have meaning. The ideals we strive for are only reflections of His attributes, and the more time we spend praying, the clearer the ideals become. Whether prayers are formal or spontaneous, spoken or silent, they are valuable in keeping us pointed in the right direction.

Though the practice should be followed right from the beginning, it's never too late to start.

* * *

The second antidote to burnout is to try to see things in perspective.

"I never think of crowds. I think only of one person," Mother Teresa once said.

In the often crushing poverty of Calcutta and around

the world, she and her nuns have managed to keep their balance by seeing only individuals. To them, Christ is not a plural noun — He lives in each person they meet.

Every long journey begins with only one step. And every problem must be approached the same way.

Each issue consists of a series of component parts that can be tackled on an individual basis. Whether we're concerned about poisonous air pollution or massive human-rights violations in various countries, we must force ourselves to focus on workable segments of the whole.

Having a realistic view of what we can achieve assists in this last. It's fine to have high ideals and great hopes for the permanent transformation of the world, but when those ideals and hopes blind us to human limitations and cause us to downgrade ourselves and the others who are working for the same purpose, they must be re-examined.

We *can't* clean up the air we breathe to a virgin state — but we *can* compel local authorities to clean up the resident smoke-belching copper smelter. We *can't* topple the entire political structure of a Central American dictatorship, but we *can* effect the release of one prisoner of conscience from its jails.

One activist who was very discouraged in her work for peace in Central America says she was turned around by this realization.

"I suddenly knew," she said, "that it was really all a case of one-to-one. Each person helping one person was the only way that world problems would be solved. And when I began to act on that idea, all my energy was renewed!"

Understanding that it doesn't all depend on one person helps, too. No crisis will be completely solved by a single person — no long-standing issue can be finally cleared up by an individual.

The heroes who've sparked major changes in the world (including Gandhi, Dorothy Day, and St. Francis of Assisi) couldn't have done it alone. Their work had to be picked up and carried on by others, and they had to know when to step back and let them take over.

We, too, need to remember that others are working for the same results, and sometimes they must be allowed to carry the bulk of the burden. We must know when to "back off" for a time. After all, no one is indispensable.

On the other hand, we must give ourselves some credit. The reason we fail so often is because we've set our sights so high. That fact should fill us with pride, not shame. Without ideals, nothing is accomplished.

* * *

There are those in the peace and justice business and other worthwhile causes who become obsessed with their objectives. They focus only on their desired ends, and whether or not they obtain them becomes a part of their very sense of self. If their work should fail, they generally react in one of two ways: they despair or become totally cynical and stop trying. Both reactions, of course, are prime symptoms of burnout.

Eknath Easwaran, one of Gandhi's biographers, addressed the problem when he said, "A person who is worried about the outcome of his work does not see his goal — he sees only his opposition and the obstacles before him. Feeling unequal to the difficulties of his situation, he becomes resigned or resorts to violence out of frustration and despair."

The obvious solution to the problem is to become detached from our perceived objectives. If we work for a cause, it must be because it's right to do so — not just because it will yield a certain result. We must do the work for its own sake.

Montaigne wrote, "It is the journey, not the arrival, that matters." And T.S. Eliot added, "For us there is only the trying. The rest is not our business."

In the Old Testament, Moses could do nothing to move Ramses when God determined that the pharaoh's heart would be hardened. No miracle could change his mind until the time was ripe for the people of Israel to be released.

We must recognize that we may be involved in a similar situation. If we can't see success, it may only be because the timing is not yet right for "our" goal to happen. Though that doesn't excuse us from continuing to try for it, it should help us relax when the failures seem to come fast and thick.

Even Mother Teresa once said that we're not called to success, but only to faithfulness.

* * *

Another way to combat the effects of burnout is to back up.

Reviewing the amount of progress we've made in a given period of time often helps to put a better face on things. And don't be cynical! Although each step forward may be small objectively, the fact is that it *is* a step and it *is* forward.

So it's valuable to occasionally reexamine what we've accomplished both in order to restore ourselves and to help us reset our course if we've gotten too far off the track.

Journal-writing is an immense help here. Diaries are dandy places to dump negative feelings as they happen, to mentally work out conflicts, and to review our situation when the going gets tough. During times when we find we've forgotten why we decided to work in the first place, a journal that records our initial enthusiasm will help us recommit ourselves. We may be surprised at how much deeper our understanding has become, and how much more profound our discernment and commitment have grown.

When the world seems a bleak spot, making no progress against the evils that beset it, we can reread history as well. Believe it or not, humanity has made a lot of headway in the last one hundred fifty years!

Human-rights agreements, the abolition of slavery, and the eradication of smallpox are only a few of the giant strides that have been accomplished, which just two centuries ago would have been unthinkable. And there's no reason to believe that further "insurmountable" problems won't be similarly conquered. None of the people working for the above had reason to believe that they would be successful any more than do today's anti-war workers, animal-rights crusaders, or ecologists.

* * *

As mentioned earlier, burnout is a temporary loss of

balance that comes from focusing on one spot too long. One way to recover from it is obviously to refocus.

Working on a different aspect of the same problem, changing methods of working, or temporarily committing ourselves to an entirely different project can revive us. As we face a wholly new set of problems and solutions, we find that those difficulties which defeated us originally regain perspective.

Those who've been teaching about human-rights abuses may discover great satisfaction in joining a letter-writing campaign dealing with religious discrimination. Or one who had been involved in a global hunger phone tree may find no problem in withdrawing from it to participate in hosting people from other lands in a hospitality project.

When and if we do return to our original field, we will bring new resources to it and will be able to see it in better relation to the whole picture.

* * *

There are times, though, when burnout becomes so severe that we must withdraw from all of our actions.

Helen Caldicott, the Australian doctor who founded Physicians for Social Responsibility, did that in 1985. She announced that she could no longer go on without respite, and that she and her husband would spend a year or so camping in the Outback of her native country.

Though most people don't have that option, there are other ways to get the same effect.

Temporarily resigning from groups, canning letters unopened from worthy organizations, and unplugging from the media are a few of them. Such actions require a great deal of willpower, but since they're vital for sanity and health, they should be considered necessary evils. Most groups will readily understand and encourage retreats from commitments.

Servas, the international hospitality organization, is one that recognizes the need for moderation in participating in its program. According to Servas's guidelines for hosts, "You must decline to accept more travelers than you can easily handle."

* * *

"Lighten up!" has become a byword in today's America, and it certainly applies to those who need to recover from overinvolvement.

Physical exercise is a great way to work out the tensions and exhaustion that go with burnout. At times, belting a punching bag, running in place, or doing some strenuous housework may be just the remedy for overwhelming frustration!

Watching a funny movie, reading a light book of fiction, or just doing something "useless" like building a jigsaw puzzle brings us a long way toward recovery. We must shelve, if we can, the feelings of guilt that may go along with these activities and withdrawals. We can adopt the attitude that they're as necessary for us as medicine is for the critically ill.

Moreover, we must be patient. It sometimes takes a long time to heal.

* * *

Finally, it's wise to understand that the best way to cope with the burnout syndrome is to prevent it.

Whether that knowledge comes as a result of going

through one bout with the problem, or from recognizing the possibility ahead of time and preparing for it, we are doing ourselves and others a favor if we take certain precautions.

We should arrange to talk out our problems and frustrations as they occur. This can be done by phone or in person, with someone in the field or with an interested friend. Problems shouldn't be left to build up.

Journal-keeping, as mentioned before, is a fine way to unload negative feelings and questions onto paper. If the emotions are terribly hostile or despairing, it may be very satisfying to shred or burn the paper after they're written down.

We must limit our involvement to what we can reasonably take. The temptation, of course, is always to accept more responsibility, more meaningful projects. But both our effectiveness and our health require that we concede to personal limitations.

Adding to our commitments slowly, then stopping when they seem to be too much, is a most effective way to continue our calling of "saving the world from our home."

13
conclusion

"And now the news..."

Objectively, TV reporters still mouth the same old gloom and doom. Newspapers still crank out columns on the imminent decline of civilization. And radio announcers still broadcast gruesome gossip of wars and anguish.

But there's a difference.

For those of us who have learned to focus our concern on small workable areas, there's hope.

We're less overwhelmed by the mass of statistics, the avalanche of information. Since we've managed to concentrate on individual projects and problems, too, we can see results more quickly than the cursory cameras do.

For those of us who have begun to educate ourselves to the reality behind the headlines, there's promise.

We know that things aren't always as black as they're painted. We've learned to see through obvious half-truths and propaganda. And we can follow stories through to possible conclusions to see that they aren't all disastrous.

For those of us who have learned to act, there's a feeling of power.

We are contributing to the actions that make the news. *We* are making the media and government more responsive to their public. *We* are preserving the best aspects of the world for those who are to come. And for those of us who've worked on developing proper attitudes, there's even joy.

Our lives have become more human in the practice of trusting one another and opening ourselves to one another. Because we have patience and trust in God, we can see things in perspective. Temporary setbacks and apparent disasters have assumed reasonable proportions.

Praying, writing, phoning, doing artwork, being hospitable, giving, joining, and the many other actions that add to the overall picture of peace and cooperation — all these are our weapons against despair. They are the tools with which we serve one another and bring about God's kingdom on earth. They, combined with faith, are the stuff of our salvation.

". . . With God, all things are possible" (Matthew 19:26). And He uses us as His instruments on earth.

No longer should the TV news be a call to despair. It should merely be a stimulus to meaningful action.

No one's excused — no one's exempt.

The majority of the work that needs to be done to change the world can be accomplished right at home. Those who are based there often have the time and opportunity not available to those in the field to make radical changes. They can use them with thanksgiving.

Needless to say, the benefits for those of us who try are numerous.

We gain a sense of power over our own lives. We become more optimistic. We know that we're needed. And we strengthen our own health in working for others.

Our energies and sense of purpose are restored.

We can agree with Dr. Roger Fisher when he writes in *The Peace Catalog*: "There is more exhilaration, more challenge, more zest in tilting at windmills than in any routine job. I see no reason to be gloomy about trying to save the world!"